VOICE OF GOD

VOICE
OF
GOD

herman h. riffel

Tyndale House
Publishers, Inc.
Wheaton, Illinois

This book is dedicated to our son, David, who has heard the voice of God and is seeking to follow it.

Library of Congress
Catalog Card Number 78-55979
ISBN 0-8423-7803-0, paper
Copyright © 1978
by Herman H. Riffel.
All rights reserved.
First printing, October 1978
Printed in the
United States of America

CONTENTS

FOREWORD

The sincere Christian knows no more important task than learning how to listen to God. How does God speak to me here and now, to give me direction, inspiration and guidance? How do I distinguish between God's voice and the other voices which speak within the inner person? Herman Riffel has addressed himself to this most important Christian concern in this important book. He deals honestly and directly with the problems of discerning the voice of God.

The author writes out of years of Christian experience as a pastor. This work is the result of a sensitive and mature spirit struggling to know God's will and direction for his life. He shares what he has learned. This study combines Christian experience, mature biblical understanding and psychological wisdom. I can recommend it to anyone who wants to listen more closely to God. It is not only theoretically sound, but down to earth and practically useful. I know of no other book which speaks so directly to this essential human concern.

Morton Kelsey
Gualala, California

FOREWORD

INTRODUCTION
The Purpose Of This Book

As we minister to Christian leaders and lay persons around the world, the question they ask most frequently is this: "How do you recognize the voice of God and distinguish it from all the other voices that we hear?"

There are many voices that demand our hearing. There is the voice of public opinion, the voice of authority, the voice of our own desires, the voice of conscience, and the many voices of the tempter. How shall we know the voice of God among all these voices? The question has an urgency about it, for the success of our ministry depends upon it. Yet the answer seems to be so mysterious.

There is nothing more basic to the church's ministry than to know what God is saying to us today. Perhaps the great difference in the results of the ministry of the early church and that of the traditional church of today lies in receiving direction for that ministry. The church of the book of The Acts of the Apostles first heard God speak and then called a meeting to decide how to carry out God's word. In contrast, in our churches of today we have business meetings to make up our strategy and then ask God to bless it, which he is often unable to do. We need to learn to hear God's voice in order to discern God's purpose among the many devious plans of the world and to find God's strategy in our conflict with the enemy.

This book is written to help remove the barriers for those who want to learn to listen to the voice of God. It offers safeguards, so that one may learn to hear God's voice reliably. It is my prayer and that of my wife, Lillie, who so richly shares in my ministry, that this book will help to bring us all into a greater maturity in discerning the voice of God.

Herman Riffel

ONE

HOW GOD SPOKE TO MAN

1
God
Did Speak
With Man

When the raging Communist army took over most of China and most foreigners had fled to the coastal cities or left the country, an American missionary wife, Isobel Kuhn, remained stranded in the interior of that vast country. Because she was a foreigner, escape was her only hope, but the routes all seemed closed. No quick modes of transportation were available to her. In her desperation, she sought God's guidance. He provided it.

After she escaped, she told how God had miraculously directed her footsteps. Her Lord showed her which routes to take, often afoot. He indicated which village was safe to stop in, even which house to stay in, and when to go. Sometimes with her pursuers right behind her, she escaped their clutches with only minutes to spare. By listening to the voice of God as he spoke to her morning by morning and hour by hour, she was able to filter through enemy lines to the coast and then back to her own land of America.

Upon hearing that story and later conversing with her about it, I said to myself, "Does God give that kind of guidance for emergencies only; or does he want to guide us that way day by day?" As I thought over the Scriptures, I decided that such guidance should be the normal experience of the Christian.

Who of us has not been frightened away from the thought of such direct guidance when we have seen tragic experiences of some people who have claimed to have it? When some said that they heard God tell them to sell all their possessions, leave everything, and wait for the Lord to come, we knew that they were *not* receiving the guidance of God. And when some made excuse for their failure to be the voice of God, we saw through their irresponsibility. Yet if there is such a thing as God's direct guidance for us, we should find it in the experiences of men and women of the Bible and also of godly people living today.

Throughout the Bible record we find men and women who heard God speak and followed him. For example the prophet Elijah, with perfect assurance told the wicked King Ahab, "As surely as the Lord God of Israel lives—the God whom I worship and serve—there won't be any dew or rain for several years until I say the word!" And there was no rain for three and a half years. Conditions became so bad that King Ahab said to Obadiah, his servant, "We must check every stream and brook to see if we can find enough grass to save at least some of my horses and mules. You go one way and I'll go the other, and we will search the entire land." Then the Lord said to Elijah again, "Go and tell King Ahab that I will soon send rain again." When Elijah had prayed he shouted, "Hurry to Ahab and tell him to get into his chariot and get down the mountain, or he'll be stopped by the rain." And sure enough, the sky was soon black with clouds, and a heavy wind brought a terrific rainstorm. (See 1 Kings 17, 18.) Elijah had indeed heard from God!

You will remember also how Moses stood before the great Egyptian Pharaoh and told him to let God's people go or God would send judgments upon him. He named the specific judgments that would come. And just as he said, so it happened. He said that if Pharaoh would not let the people go, the water would turn to blood, the fish would die, and the river would stink. Pharaoh did not relent. So it all came true—"The fish died and the water became so foul that the Egyptians couldn't drink it; and there was blood throughout the land of Egypt" (Exodus 7:21).

Moses also said God would send vast hordes of frogs— and frogs covered the nation. He said a deadly plague would destroy the cattle the next day—and the very next morning the cattle of the Egyptians began to die but the cattle of the Israelites were untouched. So accurately did Moses hear God speak, that even the Egyptians were afraid of his word.

Daniel, another prophet, stood before the great King Nebuchadnezzar and interpreted God's message that came to him through dreams. The interpretation was right, and when Nebuchadnezzar did not humble himself the judgment fell upon him just as Daniel had predicted from the dream. The king had to recognize that Daniel's word was reliable. "I know," said the king, "that the spirit of the holy gods is in you and no mystery is too great for you to solve." (See Daniel 1—4.) Thus great kings were humbled before God through the messages of men who understood and recognized the voice of God.

But while prophets such as Elijah, Moses, and Daniel were bold in their stand before men, privately they struggled with God to see if they were really hearing him rightly. Jeremiah once said to God, "Lord, you know it is for your sake that I am suffering. They are persecuting me because I have proclaimed your word to them. Don't let them kill me! Rescue me from their clutches, and give them what they deserve!—Yet you have failed me in my time of need! You have let them keep right on with all their persecution. Will they never stop hurting me? Your help is as uncertain as a seasonal mountain brook—sometimes a flood, sometimes as dry as a bone!"

To this the Lord replied: "Stop this foolishness and talk some sense! Only if you return to trusting me will I let you continue as my spokesman. You are to influence them, not let them influence *you!*" (Jeremiah 15:18, 19).

Some of those men risked their whole futures on what they felt they were hearing God say. Abraham, for example, left his home, his family, and his possessions to go to another land occupied by other peoples, expecting that God would fulfill his word. He trusted that God would give him a family and out of that family build a nation, and make that nation to bless the world. Subsequent history proved that Abraham had heard God right.

Noah built a huge ship on dry land. He did it on the basis of hearing God giving very specific plans, plans that are still valid in ship building today.

Joseph, through directions given in a dream, took Mary and the infant child and fled with them to the far-off land of Egypt. There he was protected because he acted quickly on what he heard God say in the dream. That is comparable to someone today acting on the basis of a dream to take his wife and child and before the day is over, move his family to Europe. In the morning he would get up and make reservations, and before the day was over they would be on their way to make their home in Europe.

The apostle Paul wrote letters of instruction which still serve as valid guidelines for today's churches. The apostle John received revelations of things to come through visions, and he was so sure of God's communication in those visions that he closed his book with this statement: "If anyone adds anything to what is written here, God shall add to him the plagues described in this book. And if anyone subtracts any part of these prophecies, God shall take away his share in the Tree of Life, and in the Holy City just described." (Revelation 22:18, 19).

Beyond the experience of all other men, it is important to hear what Jesus had to say about man's communication with God. Jesus, who himself was in constant communication with his heavenly Father, expected that his followers would recognize his voice. Using the illustration of the gatekeeper or shepherd, he said, "He walks ahead of them; and they follow him, for they recognize his voice. . . . They won't follow a stranger but will run from him, for they don't recognize his voice. I am the Good Shepherd and know my own sheep, and they know me. . . .My sheep recognize my voice, and I know them and they follow me" (John 10:4, 5, 14, 15, 27).

We see, then, that Jesus expects that those who are truly his followers will recognize his voice and follow him. His voice will become so familiar to them that if they hear another voice calling them aside they immediately know not to follow it, for it is not the voice of their shepherd. They follow their shepherd by the recognition of his voice.

Has God stopped speaking to man? Hear the testimony of a modern disciple of Jesus Christ in one of her many experiences of hearing from God. Corrie ten Boom tells how she heard the Lord tell her to go from Formosa to the Philippine Islands; to Auckland, New Zealand; to Sydney, Australia; to Johannesburg, South Africa; to Tel Aviv, Israel; to Barcelona, Spain; to Amsterdam, Holland. She therefore gave the airlines ticket agent the planned route but when she got her ticket the route had been changed. Corrie protested that the Lord had told her to go via the route that she had given. The clerk explained that there were no direct connections between Australia and South Africa. The distance was too great for one flight over the ocean, the plane would need an island on which to refuel. But Corrie said that the Lord had given her specific directions that she must follow. Imagine how impressed the clerk was when she learned the next day that the company had obtained landing rights on an island and the plane could now fly the exact route that God had given to Corrie. So God continues to speak to human beings.

Is there any indication in Scripture that God would cease to converse with man? Is the need to hear God not as great today as it was in those days? Surely the course of this world has not changed. The god of this world is still working in every stratum of life to lead us astray. How will the church, the body of Christ, know what to say and do unless its Head, the Lord Jesus Christ, guides it? Is there a way, then, to learn to recognize that voice and follow it safely? All these questions coming from honest doubts must be considered carefully and dealt with honestly.

We need to observe how God spoke to the men who wrote the Bible and see if their experience is a pattern for us in their communication with God. Did they too have to learn to recognize God's voice as we do, or did God communicate with them only in some special way? What were the languages in which God spoke to man? Have we lost the understanding of any of these languages, thus losing some ability to communicate with God?

From the human side we wonder about the many voices that we hear and how we hear them. How do we differentiate the voice of God from all other voices? As we consider all these questions carefully we can learn to listen to the voice of God with more confidence until we learn to recognize it. Even then we want to learn to test the guidance we get. Is it reliable enough so that we can put our whole weight on it? Last, we should find a pattern to show us how to handle the strange phenomena of the spiritual realm so that we do not get carried away. We need to relate to this world properly and yet to learn to hear the voice of God reliably, for both worlds are part of our environment. This is our task.

2
How God Spoke to the Men Who Wrote the Bible

How did God speak to men when they wrote what later became the sacred Scriptures? Was it in some mysterious way now lost in antiquity? Was it by the secret hand of God upon ancient stone? Or did these sayings and writings of the Bible come to holy prophets in ecstatic experiences too high for us to attain?

The question is important. We need to know: were the Bible writers' experiences once-in-history experiences, or does God speak to men today as he spoke then? To find the answer we must examine how God spoke to those who became writers of that composite material which we now call the Holy Bible.

Many of us have only a vague concept of how the Bible was written. If that concept were to be described it would sound as if the Bible came to us by magic. We seem to feel that in some mysterious way the Scriptures came to man about the way the law came to Moses, through angels on Mt. Sinai. But instead we find that the Scriptures, when given, were records of experiences that happened to men and were recorded for the occasion.

We know that the apostle Paul said, "All scripture is inspired by God and can profitably be used for teaching, for refuting error, for guiding peoples' lives and teaching them to be holy" (2 Timothy 3:16 JB). And we remember that the apostle Peter said, "No prophecy ever came from man's initiative. When men spoke for God it was the Holy Spirit that moved them" (2 Peter 1:21 JB). Peter had also said in his first letter that the Spirit of Christ which was in the prophets had spoken through them. And then he said that the same Holy Spirit who moved the prophets to write also moved men and women to preach the gospel to the scattered Christians.

We may be surprised to find that the writers of the Bible were normal people like you and me, seemingly moved or inspired by the Holy Spirit as we too may be. Some were men of great faith, like Moses, Samuel, and David. Some were prophets who had had such experiences with God that, like Elijah, they were able to stand up to powerful kings. Some, like Isaiah, had messages to the great nations of Egypt, Babylonia, and Assyria. And some were highly trained men like Saul the Pharisee, a member of the Jewish Sanhedrin, who later became the apostle Paul. But there were also common men like the herdsman Amos, the fishermen John and Peter, and the tax collector Matthew. The writers include a wise man, Solomon, who became foolish in his later life and wrote some things from that low level of experience. They also include a disobedient prophet, Jonah, who apparently wrote after trying to run away from God. Then too there were Jesus' brothers, who had not believed in him while he was part of their household but only later came to believe in him and then wrote part of what we now know as the Holy Scriptures.

The authors of the books of the Bible wrote historical records for their time. They wrote songs for worship and love songs. They gathered proverbs and gave many great prophecies from God. In the New Testament we have four records of the life of Jesus, one of whose writers (Luke the physician) provides a sequel—the history of the early church. All the rest of the New Testament contains personal letters to churches, or to scattered Christians, or to individuals.

These men, then, wrote as would modern historians, song writers, or correspondents. When Moses gave Israel the Ten Commandments he received from God with all the details of the Law, he put them into their historical setting. He told of the failings of Abraham, Isaac, and Jacob. He records his own arguments with God when God called him. He describes the rebellion of Israel and how the Law was given to them. He even tells how in his later life he failed and therefore could not enter the promised land. He wrote out of his own imperfection, though what he wrote was preserved to become the Scriptures for us.

So also Moses wrote down for Israel the Law that God had given to him; but with that Law he also gave a very careful account of Israel's history from the beginning. He even went back to the origin of man and the story of creation, which he received by revelation. As a great leader he left a careful history for his nation, Israel. So also Joshua, his successor, and Samuel and David and Ezra and Isaiah and many others continued that history.

The Psalms, all with the "ring of truth" in them, were written as songs and as prayers, often in the time of trouble. The third Psalm comes out of great travail when David with his army is fleeing barefoot from his son. Absalom was staging a coup to usurp his father's kingdom. In the psalm David says, "O Lord, so many are against me. So many seek to harm me. I have so many enemies. So many say that God will never help me. But Lord, you are my shield, my glory, and my only hope. You alone can lift my heart, now bowed in shame. I cried out to the Lord, and he heard me from his Temple in Jerusalem. Then I lay down and slept in peace and woke up safely, for the Lord was watching over me. And now, although ten thousand enemies surround me on every side, I am not afraid" (Psalm 3:1-6). It's no wonder that that psalm, written in a time of trouble, speaks to so many of us in our times of difficulty.

But in the midst of the psalmists' praises come the curses that they put upon enemies—curses which do not all agree with the spirit of Jesus. "May his children become fatherless and his wife a widow," says one psalm, which goes on to say, "May they be evicted from the ruins of their home. May creditors seize his entire estate and strangers take all he has earned. Let no one be kind to him; let no one pity his fatherless children. May they die" (Psalm 109:9-12). Another goes so far as to say, "Blessed is the man who takes your babies and smashes them against the rocks!" (Psalm 137:9). Shocking thoughts to find in the Bible! But are they not the same kinds of thoughts that sometimes come to our minds in the midst of our worship and praise to God? The psalmists were the same kind of men as we are.

The prophets too, spoke for the occasion. The introduction to the prophecy of Isaiah is as follows: "These are the messages that came to Isaiah, son of Amos, in the visions he saw during the reigns of King Uzziah, King Jotham, King Ahaz and King Hezekiah—all kings of Judah. In these messages God showed him what was going to happen to Judah and Jerusalem in the days ahead.

"Listen, O heaven and earth, to what the Lord is saying: The children I raised and cared for so long and tenderly have turned against me" (Isaiah 1:1, 2). And in the introduction to Nahum's prophecy we read, "This is the vision God gave to Nahum, who lived in Elkosh, concerning the impending doom of Nineveh" (Nahum 1:1). In fact, the messages of the prophets and the songs of the psalmists come more to life when you read them in relation to their historical context—the times, the places, the kinds of rulers who were in power at a given time.

For a great portion of the church, the thirty-nine books that we call the Old Testament constituted the complete Bible of that time. After 400 years, is it any wonder that there was so much objection to adding anything to it? But when Jesus came and proved himself to be the Messiah, Matthew carefully recorded the life of Jesus and tied it right into the old historical records, mainly for the benefit of the Jewish believers of that day. John, the beloved disciple, recorded the spiritual inspiration of Jesus' teaching and his death and resurrection for whoever would read it. Mark wrote a shorter record, possibly for those outside the church. And Luke, the physician, carefully recorded the details of Jesus' life according to his research and observation. None of these men seemed to be thinking of adding to the Bible, but were making careful records for their generation.

Luke wrote to Theophilus, "Dear Friend who loves God: Several biographies of Christ have already been written using as their source material the reports circulating among us from the early disciples and other eyewitnesses. However, it occurred to me that it would be well to recheck all these accounts from first to last and after thorough investigation to pass this summary on to you, to reassure you of the truth of all you were taught" (Luke 1:1-4). Then when he wrote what we call the Acts of the Apostles, he began by saying, "Dear Friend who loves God: In my first letter I told you about Jesus' life and teachings and how he returned to heaven after giving his chosen apostles further instructions from the Holy Spirit" (Acts 1:1, 2). He then went on to show what were the results of the training that Jesus gave to his disciples when they and others received the power of the Holy Spirit that had been promised. In it he gave a very careful record of the development of the church from its Jewish beginning under the leadership of Peter to its worldwide outreach among the Gentiles through the apostle Paul. Undoubtedly this record was soon recognized to be of universal value, though Luke himself was presenting careful evidence to one man who he knew should have it.

Then follow the letters of the missionary Paul who writes very specifically "to all of you in Rome," and "to the congregation of God's people in Corinth," and "to the Christian congregations of Galatia," and "to God's people at Ephesus," and "to all those of God's people who live at Philippi," and "to God's people at Colosse." To another church he writes, "See that it is also read to the congregation at Laodicea," and to still another he writes, "to the congregation of the Thessalonians." Besides that he writes some personal letters to a young man to whom he says, "Timothy, you are like a son to me in the things of the Lord." He also writes a letter to Titus; and one to "Philemon, our dear friend and fellow worker, and Apphia—and the congregation at your house." There is no apparent indication that Paul expected any of these letters to become part of the Scriptures.

Paul even quotes the words of Jesus on one level and then gives his personal opinion on a lower level, in 1 Corinthians 7:10, 12. Because of that, C. S. Lewis, that great Christian apologist says, "Generalizing thus, I take it that the whole Old Testament consists of the same sort of material as any other literature—chronicles, poems, moral and political diatribes, romances, and what not; but all taken into the service of God's word. Not all, I suppose, in the same way. There are prophets who write with the clearest awareness that Divine compulsion is upon them. There are chroniclers whose intention may have been merely to record. There are poets like those in the Songs of Songs who probably never dreamed of any but a secular and natural purpose in what they composed."

The writers of the Bible wrote from their imperfect level of experience, as we do. God accepted their imperfections amidst their praise to God, as he does with us. How all of this became the Word of God to us we will see later. Not one of the writers of the Bible ever seemed to have thought that his historical record, or song, or personal letter, or even prophecy would become part of the Scriptures for all the future generations. In fact, their writings did not actually become part of the Bible until many years or generations or sometimes centuries after it was written. I suppose that the apostle Paul would have been shocked to find that the letter that he wrote to the Corinthians out of a dire need to defend himself would become a permanent part of God's Word. In part of that letter he wrote, "You have made me act like a fool—boasting like this—for you people ought to be writing about me and not making me write about myself. There isn't a single thing these other marvelous fellows have that I don't have too, even though I am really worth nothing at all.

When I was there I certainly gave you every proof that I was truly an apostle, sent to you by God himself; for I patiently did many wonders and signs and mighty works among you" (2 Corinthians 12:11, 12). How could he imagine that that would become part of a sacred book, enclosed in a leather cover and marked Holy Bible? He was embarrassed enough to have to write it to them at all.

Wouldn't he have been surprised to learn that personal greetings such as these that he wrote to his Roman friends would be read around the world as part of the Scriptures for two thousand years: "To my good friend Epanetus" . . . "Remember me to Mary, too" . . . "Andronicas and Julias, my relatives—please give them my greetings" . . . "Say hello to Ampliatus and Urbanus and beloved Stachys."

It was true that the words of the apostle Paul, when he had carried on such an extensive and effective ministry, were counted as important so that even Peter compares them to the value of the Old Testament books (2 Peter 3:15, 16). Yet it did not seem to Paul that he was writing something that would become part of the Bible. He knew that he was speaking under the guidance of the Holy Spirit, but so was he when he preached sermons that never became part of the Scriptures. In other words, the inspiration that came to the apostle in his preaching was the same that came in his writing. In one of his letters he says, "I do not want you to think of me as someone who only frightens you by letter. Someone said, 'He writes powerful and strongly worded letters, but when he is with you you see only half a man and no preacher at all.' The man who said that can remember this: Whatever we are like in the words of our letters when we are absent, that is what we shall be like in our actions when we are present" (2 Corinthians 10:9-11 JB). In the preceding paragraph, describing his coming to them, he said, "Though we walk in the flesh, we do not war after the flesh: (For the weapons of our warfare are not carnal, but mighty through God to the pulling down of strongholds;) casting down imaginations, and every high thing that exalteth itself against the knowledge of God, and bringing into captivity every thought to the obedience of Christ; and having a readiness to revenge all disobedience, when your obedience is fulfilled" (2 Corinthians 10:3-6 KJV). So you see the apostle wrote as being led by the Holy Spirit in the same way he was empowered by the Spirit in his preaching and in his daily actions. There is no indication of a special revelation when he wrote things that became part of the Bible, other than what he had by the Spirit of God as he spoke.

James wrote to "the twelve tribes dispersed throughout the world" (James 1:1 NEB). Peter wrote "to those of God's scattered people who lodged for a while at Pontus, Galatia, Cappadocia, Asia and Bithynia" (1 Peter 1:1 NEB). The first letter of John seems to be more general, yet it is designated as a letter, probably to some churches. Then he wrote a very personal letter, "to that dear woman Cyria, one of God's very own, and to her children whom I love so much, as does everyone else in the church," and another letter, "Dear Gaius, whom I truly love." And in what we call the book of Revelation, John wrote specifically, "to the seven churches in the Province of Asia" (Ephesus, Smyrna, Pergamos, Thyatira, Sardis, Philadelphia, and Laodicea).

We see the difference of revelation in the New Testament over against the Old as the writer of the book of Hebrews says, "Long ago God spoke in many different ways to our fathers through the prophets (in visions, dreams, and even face to face), telling them little by little about his plans. But now in these days he has spoken to us through his Son to whom he has given everything, and through whom he made the world and everything there is" (Hebrews 1:1, 2). In the Old Testament we see various prophets standing out like stars in the night sky, but in the New Testament we see Jesus like the blazing mid-day sun. All the prophecy is centered in him. This does not mean that after Jesus came others did not prophesy, for they did. Nor that guidance was not given through dreams and visions, for it often was. Nor does it mean that the Holy Spirit may not use any means to speak to us, for the apostles still wrote their letters to specific people on definite occasions. But after Jesus came we no longer see one great prophet after another, but rather we see Jesus manifesting himself through the Spirit who speaks in many ways, often seemingly insignificant ways, through persons and conversations and letters that originally seemed rather ordinary but came to be extremely meaningful for people of all cultures and of every succeeding generation.

If the records made were for their times, and if the songs were for the occasions of their celebration, and if the letters were to the specific churches and individuals, we may wonder how they became part of the Bible—part of what we call the canon of Scripture. The word *canon* comes from the Latin referring to a rule or rod, such as is used by masons or carpenters. It had reference to measuring. Thus the canon of Scripture has come to refer to the recognized books which we call the Bible. It is the rule of measurement for us to go by. The collective experiences of man with God as found in these books have become the rule for us to go by.

How were these books selected from all others? There were other sacred records kept, there were many other good songs written, and we know that Paul wrote other letters not included in the canon; but an important process established the canon. It is a process that was applied to the greatest books of the Bible as well as to the simplest recorded experience of a believer receiving his message from God. The apostle Paul applied that principle to the prophecies in the Corinthian church. "Of the prophets," he said, "two or three may speak, while the rest exercise their judgment upon what is said" (1 Corinthians 14:29 NEB). By this means the church is to discern whether a prophecy is of God or merely of the prophet himself. That principle was applied by God's children universally, to each individual prophecy, so that the church over all, through a long period of time, discerned among many writings which of them was indeed of God. Those writings became a part of the canon of Scripture.

First the Jews made a collection of books until over a period of centuries they had gathered the books that were universally recognized as canonical. Then the process began all over again with the New Testament writings. Some of the books were not accepted for a long time. Some were accepted almost immediately. However, the universal process was at work. As Henry C. Thiessen says, "It is a remarkable fact that no early church council selected the books which should constitute the New Testament canon. The books that we now have crushed out all rivals not by any advantageous authority but by their own weight and worth."[1] And as F. F. Bruce says, "The first time that a church council promulgated a statement about which books made up the New Testament canon was in A.D. 393. That council was merely a provincial synod in North Africa. It perpetrated no innovation but simply recognized the situation which had been established by Christian use and want over the preceding two hundred years and more. Inclusion in the canon conferred on no book an authority which it did not already possess. The books were included in the canon because of the authority which was accorded to them individually throughout the Christian world from the end of the first century onward."[2] We will see later why this process of discernment is so valid and reliable.

Perhaps we would like to have a more perfect Bible, in the sense that it is without the record of all the human experiences of frailty and error; we'd like it all in the format of a perfect standard, like the Ten Commandments. But if it were so, would we not quickly feel condemned by our human limitations in comparison to such perfection? God has chosen instead to provide accounts of the experiences of humans with their frailties and imperfections as the test and guide for our walk with God.

God brings the supernatural right into the natural. Think of the mystery of the incarnation—God becoming manifest in a human body. So it is also with the Scriptures. God gives his Word by his Spirit and it is spoken by frail, sinful flesh; yet it becomes a very word of God to man. As C. S. Lewis aptly says, "We are taught that the Incarnation itself proceeds 'not by the conversion of the godhead into flesh, but taking of (the) manhood of God'; in it human life becomes the vehicle of Divine life." So, he continues, "the Scriptures proceed not by conversion of God's word into a literature but by taking up of a literature to be a vehicle of God's word."[3]

If God so spoke when he gave the Scriptures to man, then he can still be speaking in the same way. Does that mean, then, that we can all add our own bit to the sacred Scriptures? Suppose that someone says he will add to a book, or to a letter or a song of the Scriptures. That is unthinkable in view of the fact that none even of the Bible writers themselves ever pretended to do that. They wrote for the occasion. Its becoming part of the Scriptures was not by their decision but by the Holy Spirit's, made clear in the church over generations and centuries. So we are not even to think of adding or subtracting anything from the Bible. In fact it is amazing that God should choose to take any of the imperfect experiences of men and give them such a high position and enduring quality as to make them a part of the Word of God to all men for centuries afterwards. But we do recognize that God spoke in very natural ways to the men who wrote the Bible.

Let us see if their way of hearing God was as natural as God's way of speaking to them.

3
Did These Men Hear God Perfectly?

When we read the writings of the authors of the Bible who spoke to kings, composed immortal songs of praise, and penned letters that have guided our churches for nearly two thousand years, we stand in awe of their ability to hear from God. But have you ever wondered whether those authors of the Bible always heard God perfectly? Did they always understand him correctly?

If these authors all had the unique experience of always receiving the messages of God perfectly, we would certainly thank God for the messages and yet we would learn nothing from their experiences. On the other hand, if those people's listening was not perfect, that fact would encourage us in our own listening. If even they had to *learn* to listen, then we can take heart and learn also.

Let us look carefully into the record of these men and women who believed and obeyed God, looking not to diminish their position, but to see those things that tell us that they were like us. Then we too can learn to listen to God as they did.

We find that, just as today, there was a prejudice against many who said they were hearing from God. We remember that the older sister and brother of Moses complained, saying, "Has the Lord spoken only through Moses? Hasn't he spoken through us, too?" (Numbers 12:2). When God heard the complaint and called them before him, he said concerning Moses, "That is not how I communicate with my servant Moses. He is completely at home in my house! With him I speak face to face! And he shall see the very form of God! Why then were you not afraid to criticize him?" (Numbers 12:7, 8). Who would dare to complain against such a great prophet? But prejudice and pride blinded eyes then as it does today.

Amaziah, the king of Israel, said to another prophet, "Get out of here, you prophet, you! Flee to the land of Judah and do your prophesying there! Don't bother us here with your visions, not here in the capital, where the king's chapel is!" (Amos 7:12, 13). Amos responded to the king by saying that he was not really one of the prophets. He was a herdsman with no other ambition. But the Lord had taken him from the flocks and told him to go and prophesy to his people Israel. The hand of the Lord was upon him and he had to go. Furthermore the authority of the Lord was also with him and he predicted terrible things for the king and his family. The proof of the prophet lay not in the position given him by man but in the authority of his message and its fulfillment. Therefore the prejudice of man could not destroy his message. His position may be high or low in the eyes of man and yet be acceptable to God.

James, speaking of the greatest of the prophets, said, "Elijah was as completely human as we are" (James 5:17). Elijah and all the other prophets had to *learn to hear* God, just as we do. Think how Samuel, one of the great prophets of Israel's early history, learned to recognize God's voice. Brought to the temple as a child, he had no one to teach him to know the voice of God in the temple. Even Eli, the priest, did not know that voice. During that time of spiritual drought for Israel, messages from God were very rare. But then a most unusual thing happened. Here is the story. One night after Eli had gone to bed Samuel heard a voice calling, "Samuel, Samuel."

Samuel jumped up and ran to Eli saying, "Here I am. What do you want?"

Eli, not being familiar with the voice of God, said to Samuel, "I didn't call you. Go back to bed."

Again Samuel heard God calling him and again he ran to the priest because he had never heard the voice of the Lord before. But Eli just sent him back to bed. When this happened the third time, Eli finally realized that it was the Lord who had called Samuel.

It was then that the priest gave young Samuel a clue to starting communication with God. He said to Samuel, "Go and lie down again, and if he calls again, say, 'Yes Lord, I'm listening.'" So Samuel went back to bed (1 Samuel 3:9).

When Samuel heard the call of his name, he answered and God began to talk to him. That still today is the way communication begins. When God speaks we are to answer him. Samuel learned to recognize the voice of God in the same way that we may learn. Sequel: "And all Israel from Dan to Beer-sheba knew that Samuel was going to be a prophet of the Lord. Then the Lord began to give messages to him there at the Tabernacle in Shiloh, and he passed them on to the people of Israel" (1 Samuel 3:20, 21; 4:1).

The prophets held key positions in Israel. They were to be listened to as persons whose message came from God. In fact God once warned, "I will personally deal with anyone who will not listen to him and heed his messages from me." But God knew that there would be those who would try to make *themselves* prophets, so he also said; "Any prophet who falsely claims that his message is from me shall die. And any prophet who claims to give a message from other gods must die." Then God explained to them how they could tell whether a prophecy was from God or not. He said, "If the thing he prophesies doesn't happen, it is not the Lord who has given him the message; he has made it up himself. You have nothing to fear from him" (Deuteronomy 18:19-22).

This was a very important principle, but let us see how this principle of the law worked out in life. Did it always mean that the prophet whose prophecy failed was a false prophet?

Nathan was a prophet of the Lord in the court of King David. One day, David said to Nathan the prophet, "Look! Here I am living in this beautiful cedar palace while the Ark of God is out in a tent!" And Nathan replied, "Go ahead with what you have in mind, for the Lord is with you" (2 Samuel 7:2, 3). Nathan had agreed with David's good desire to build a temple for the Lord and told him so. But that night the Lord said to Nathan, "Tell my servant David not to do it!" (2 Samuel 7:4, 5). Nathan had given the king wrong advice. Apparently his affirmative reply to the king was his own first reaction to David's desire to build a temple. It was not God's word. What did that mean for a prophet? Was he a false prophet? Was he disbarred from office? No, he had made a mistake. He accepted the correction and God continued to use him. He was not a false prophet but a prophet of God who had made a mistake.

According to the law, there was a world of difference between the two. A false prophet was to be killed because the source of his information was the enemy, Satan, who would seek to lead the people astray (See Deuteronomy 13:5). But God knew and so did King David that a true prophet may make a mistake, receive correction and still be a prophet of the Lord.

We read of one prophet who was deceived by another. God allowed him to suffer for it but he still was recognized as a prophet of the Lord. The event took place during the reign of one of the most wicked kings of Israel, Jeroboam. The courage of the prophet was great. When Jeroboam went to worship at his golden calf idol, this unnamed prophet came up to the king and called out a judgment against the priest of that altar. As a sign he said the altar would split apart. The king was furious. Pointing to the prophet, he told the guards to arrest him. Instantly the king's arm was paralyzed in its outstretched position, and just then the altar split apart. The king begged the prophet to ask God to restore his arm. The prophet prayed and the king's arm was restored. Whereupon the king invited him to the palace, but the prophet said to the king, "Even if you gave me half your palace, I wouldn't go into it; nor would I eat or drink even water in this place! For the Lord has given me strict orders not to eat anything or drink any water while I'm here, and not to return to Judah by the road I came on" (1 Kings 13:8, 9). The prophet then went back another way.

Now there was an old man who heard what the prophet had done. He quickly got his donkey and went after him and invited him home to dinner. The prophet did not accept the invitation because of the strict orders he had received from the Lord. But the old man replied, "I am a prophet too, just as you are; and an angel gave me a message from the Lord. I am to take you home with me and give you food and water." This word of the old man was a lie, but apparently the prophet was deceived by it, thinking that the old man had received a more recent message from the Lord. So he accepted the invitation. While they were at the table a message from the Lord came to the old man and he shouted to the prophet. "The Lord says that because you have been disobedient to his clear command, and have come here, and have eaten and drunk water in the place he told you not to, therefore your body shall not be buried in the grave of your fathers."

The record says that after the meal the prophet started on his way when a lion attacked and killed him for his disobedience. Yet the old man afterwards said to his sons concerning the prophet, "The Lord told him to shout against the altar in Bethel, and his curse against the shrines in the cities of Samaria shall surely be fulfilled." (See 1 Kings 13:1-32). The old man recognized that he had been a true prophet though he had been deceived and was disobedient. The prophets of the Lord were subject to the same tests that we are. They were accountable to God. And like us they found that God is not only just but also merciful.

Even Moses failed to hear clearly or to obey rightly the command that God gave him. A sad event took place after a mob formed in rebellion against him and Aaron because there was not enough water to drink. Moses and Aaron had become so identified with God that the people blamed them for the lack of water. So the two brothers fell before the Lord and God said to Moses, "Get Aaron's rod; then you and Aaron must summon the people. As they watch, speak to that rock over there and tell it to pour out its water. You will give them water from a rock, enough for all the people and all their cattle!" Moses took the rod, gathered the people, and said, "Listen, you rebels! Must we bring you water from this rock?" Then, probably in the heat of his anger, he struck the rock twice instead of speaking to it as he had been told to do. However, water gushed out of the rock anyway, and the people and the cattle drank. But then God said to Moses, "Because you did not believe me and did not sanctify me in the eyes of the people of Israel, you shall not bring them into the land I have promised them." (See Numbers 20:6-12.)

What a terrible disappointment that was to Moses. But did that act of disobedience mean that Moses was not a great prophet? Not at all. A eulogy at his death said, "There has never been another prophet like Moses, for the Lord talked to him face to face. And at God's command he performed amazing miracles which have never been equaled." (See Deuteronomy 34:10-12.) Not even the greatest of these prophets were perfect, nor did they hear God perfectly all the time.

Even Paul, the great apostle, who was sent by Jesus Christ himself, did not always fully hear the Lord concerning his direction. At one time Paul seemed only to hear the Holy Spirit say *no;* not *yes.* Paul had taken Silas to be his companion instead of Barnabas. They apparently wanted to go into the Turkish province of Asia, but the Spirit forbade them. Next they wanted to go north into Bithynia, but the Spirit of Jesus said *no.* This was probably quite frustrating to Paul, who had had such wonderful direction from the Lord. Some Bible scholars think the apostle had lost some of his sensitivity at the time, because of the irritation that came over the difference of opinion between him and Barnabas. We know how irritations such as those that come up between husband

and wife, or between companions who work together, make it hard for them to hear the Lord. But that night Paul had a vision through which he received his guidance. It seems that in sleep one's thoughts are shut off and his heart is free to listen. Here the irritations of Paul's mind were quieted while he slept, and through a vision he was able to get his next direction from God. (See Acts 16:6-10.)

In the life of the great apostle Paul another occasion raises a question in our minds as to who was hearing God correctly. Luke, a fellow traveler with Paul at that time, records: "We went ashore, found the local believers, and stayed with them a week. These disciples warned Paul—the Holy Spirit prophesying through them—not to go to Jerusalem." Then they came to the home of Philip the evangelist where Agabus, the prophet, visited them. He took Paul's belt, tied his own hands and feet with it, and said, "The Holy Spirit declares, 'So shall the owner of this belt be bound by the Jews in Jerusalem and turned over to the Romans.' " Quite naturally Paul's companions and the local believers begged Paul not to go to Jerusalem. But he said, "Why all this weeping? You are breaking my heart! For I am ready to die for the sake of the Lord Jesus." When the believers could not dissuade Paul they surrendered for the will of the Lord to be done. (See Acts 21:10-14.)

Evidently, someone was not hearing the Lord clearly. Either the believers who had warned Paul, or the apostle himself who was determined to go on to Jerusalem, or the people who were moved by their feelings for him, wanting to protect him. In fact, the Bible gives us no clear answer as to who was right. We just know that God continued to lead the apostle. If the people were right in saying that Paul should not go to Jerusalem (for Luke said that the Holy Spirit was prophesying through them—v. 4), then Paul was wrong in going. But if that was so, we know that God forgave Paul and continued to use him. If Paul was right, feeling that he had to go on to Jerusalem, then the word was a warning to prepare him for the trouble ahead. God overruled their mistakes as he overrules ours, and continued to use them as he continues to use us.

Once God even gave a great prophecy of blessing to Israel through a man who, for selfish purposes, was seeking to curse them. That man was Balaam, a former prophet of the Lord. Balaam knew how to get his message from God, but now he faced a great temptation. The king of Midian, who wanted to defeat Israel, offered Balaam high honor and any amount of money if he would curse Israel. God had already warned Balaam, "Don't do it!" God told him, "You are not to curse them, for I have blessed them!" (Numbers 22:12). But Balaam thought he could still squeeze a curse from God upon Israel so that he could get his gold. Three times he went to Balak's altar to seek a curse. But God gave him only a blessing for Israel. Finally he gave up, for he knew God wanted to bless and not curse. Any man who tampers with the message that God has given becomes subject to God's judgment, as Balaam did. (See Deuteronomy 31:8.) Yet, in spite of that, the message that Balaam gave to Israel stood as a great blessing and promise to that nation.

In the history of Jeremiah, that mighty prophet of God, we have a most encouraging lesson for our help. Jeremiah had stood before kings and said with authority, "The Lord says . . ."—and what he predicted would happen. However he, too, had to listen to God and receive confirmation for that which he heard from the Lord as we do. He tells about it in his book. (See Jeremiah 32:1-6.)

It was during the time that Jeremiah was imprisoned in the dungeon beneath the palace, while the Babylonian army was besieging Jerusalem, that a word from the Lord came to him. It was a most unlikely word to act upon, for Jeremiah had been imprisoned for prophesying that the city would be conquered by the king of Babylon. Now that the city was being attacked, he received a specific word saying that his cousin, Hanameel, would come and offer to sell him the farm that he owned in Anathoth, for it was Jeremiah's right to buy it. Sure enough, Hanameel came just as the Lord had said, saying, "Buy my field in Anathoth, in the land of Benjamin, for the law gives you the first right to purchase it." Then follows the little statement that is most significant to us. "Then I knew for sure that the message I had heard was really from the Lord."

He knew for sure (though he had said so earlier) only when it was confirmed by Hanameel's coming. Isn't that just like the many times that we think we have heard from the Lord but are not altogether sure? Then comes a confirmation and we are encouraged. So the great prophet Jeremiah also had to have confirmation at times before he knew for sure that he was receiving the word of the Lord. All of the great prophets heard God speak, but they did not hear perfectly.

One man, Manoah, was annoyed by the fact that his wife was hearing from an angel but he wasn't. So he prayed that God would send the angel back to give more instructions about the child that God was giving them. The Lord answered his prayer but the angel came back to his wife and not to him. She called her husband, but the angel told him that they were to follow the instructions he had given his wife, seemingly paying little attention to him. This was probably due to the fact that she had better communication with the Lord than did her husband, for she understood the Lord when the angel disappeared in a flame of fire.

"We will die," Manoah cried out to his wife, "for we have seen God!"

But his wife said, "If the Lord were going to kill us he wouldn't have accepted our burnt offerings and wouldn't have appeared to us and told us this wonderful thing and done these miracles" (Judges 13:22, 23). God did not always appear to the person who was most important in the eyes of man. And there were prejudices against the seemingly unimportant people who heard from God, just as there are today.

All who heard from God needed encouragement, correction, reproof, or confirmation, just as we do. This encourages us to listen to the voice of God. In fact, if God speaks, we had better listen. And as we shall see, if he speaks in languages that we do not understand, we had better learn the language.

TWO

GOD'S MEANS OF COMMUNI-CATION

4
The Languages in Which God Speaks

Mention the languages of God, and a person from an ethnic background may remember a childhood experience. If he is of Swedish origin he knows, of course, that God speaks Swedish and that will be the language of heaven. If he is of Italian origin he knows that Italian is God's language. We in the English-speaking world make English the universal language. But instead of the languages of nations let us think of language as any means of expressing or communicating thought.

The Aristotelian philosophy which permeates our western world's thinking confines knowledge to the five senses and reason. We question any communication that does not fit into those categories. By this philosophy we have limited even our religious experience to the confines of a narrow science of the past. We have lived in a space-time box. But now even the modern sciences of physics and mathematics are no longer limited to the space-time theory. We can surely believe that God is not thus confined. God's ways of speaking are at least as numerous as man's ways of hearing.

Take the experience of a Russian soldier in the modern Soviet army who though a Christian was not limited to this rationalistic philosophy. Let's see if his experience does not compare with the experiences of various men in the Bible. Then let's see if we can enlarge our capacity to hear and see and feel and touch God, and even to smell the heavenly aroma beyond the limitations that the philosophy of this world has put upon us.

See how God encouraged Ivan, the Russian soldier, who tried to live an honest Christian life in the Soviet army in 1971 and 1972. When other soldiers asked him questions he answered them. When the officers tried to silence him and found that they could not, they beat him, jailed him, and put him out into the snow to suffer. Hear how God spoke to him and encouraged him:

> *Although the regulation bunk beds were only two feet wide and hard, Ivan stretched out between sheets and beneath a blanket and thanked God for the luxury. For the first time in 1971 he was in bed. No hours in the cold. No interrogations in the snow, in the officers' rooms. No watching the moon set behind the tiny park in the central square. Even before taps were sounded, Ivan was blissfully asleep.*
>
> *Although he had only heard it once before, the Voice was so familiar, Ivan was instantly awake. "Vanya, arise!" In a second he was on his feet between the bunks gazing at the crystal brilliance of the angel. His mind was working rapidly. He was aware that no sleeping soldier in the rows of bunks stirred. Mechanically he began to pull on his trousers and feel for his shoes, his eyes never leaving the radiant loveliness of the being before him. The angel's gaze was so full of love he felt no fear. In an instant they began to rise, and effortlessly the ceiling opened and then the barrack's roof, and Ivan and the angel flew through time and space to another world.*

The grass was deep and lush and seemed to stretch to the very horizon of this unfamiliar planet. It was a fresh and vivid green. Dazed, Ivan followed the angel, and after what seemed to be a long time they came to a brook. Its waters were as clear as glass so Ivan could see the bed of the stream, and the brightness of the water dazzled his eyes. . . .

In the brilliance of this world, every detail of blade of grass and petal of flower stood out as if floodlit. . . . The expanse of the branches were profoundly graceful, so luminous that the light seemed to pour from within each tree. Instinctively, Ivan lifted his eyes to the sky, gazing in every direction. There was no sun.

When his eyes returned to the angel, there was a form beside the being, more **exalted** and at the same time somehow more loving in his brilliance than even the angel. In some way the angel seemed to do him deference, and Ivan knew him to be the apostle John. Through the angel, the apostle communicated with him. Ivan stood transfixed, his mind absorbing every holy word. A series of three beings followed the apostle, recognized in some mysterious way by Ivan to be David, Moses, and Daniel. So intense was Ivan's concentration and so overwhelming his awe and joy that when the last form was gone Ivan felt he would fall into a deep sleep. But the angel, now alone in the streaming light, spoke again.

"We have traveled a long way and you are tired. Come and sit."

The tree under which Ivan sat was large and welcoming, with a fragrance that reminded him in some unexplained way of the grape fields of Moldavia. If the angel had not spoken again Ivan felt he would be content to sit forever, smelling the tree and looking at the landscape in the sparkling light.

"I wish to show you the heavenly city, the new Jerusalem. But if you see it as it is, you cannot remain in the body you now have. And there is still much work for you left on earth." There seemed a silence before the angel resumed speaking. "We will fly together to

another planet and I will show you the light of this city
for you to know, while you are yet alive in your earth
body, that in certainty there is a new Jerusalem." . . .

At the first glance Ivan recoiled in dismay. The brilliance was so intense that even though he had seen it
only for a second, he was sure he had been blinded. The
angel spoke immediately. "Nothing will happen to you.
Look."

No man rescued from a desert ever drank water
more thirstily than Ivan drank in the splendor of that
light. So great was its power, it could be felt, tasted,
heard. The sight of it was not a sensation of his eyes, but
of his whole heart and being. Ivan could have wept with
grief and disappointment when the angel said, "The
time has come to fly back to earth."

At the instant that Ivan's feet touched the floor beside his bunk, three things happened. The angel disappeared, the bugle for reveille sounded, and the lights in
the room snapped on. Staring stupidly at his neat bed
and himself fully dressed, Ivan heard a gentle laugh
from the bunk beside him. Grigorii Fedorovich Chernykh, his neighbor, was also a Moldavian and took a
fraternal interest in his strange countryman. Now
Chernykh was pulling himself expertly out of his bunk
and shoving his feet into trouser legs as he whispered in
a conspiratorial tone, "Vanya, where were you last
night?"

With a tremendous effort Ivan pulled his thoughts
together. The barrack was alive with bodies hurtling
past his bunk to the door. Goodnatured bantering, the
groaning of exhausted soldiers, the flash of uniforms
seemed unreal. He turned to look intently at Chernykh.

"You don't mean that you didn't see me getting un-
dressed and into bed last night? We turned in at the
same time."

Chernykh was buttoning his shirt rapidly. "You
went to bed the same time I did, all right, and to sleep,
too. But you didn't sleep long. I woke up about three A.M.
and your bunk was empty. Vanya, you were nowhere in

*this room." Reaching for his jacket, he gave Ivan a sly
smile. "Of all people, did you actually go A.W.O.L. last
night?"*

*He had not been dreaming! He had journeyed with
the angel! Excitement tore through Ivan like electricity.
They were moving hurriedly to the door.*

*His voice shook as he spoke. "Let's ask the duty offi-
cer if anyone left during the night."*

*The duty officer was indignant. "Certainly no one
left the room. Get going! Are you trying to get me arrested?!"*

*Ivan and Grigorii Chernykh moved out into the
morning, both in silence. Finally Chernykh broke the
spell of strangeness with a question and Ivan began to
tell him about the angel.*[4]

This amazing experience of Ivan's makes us wonder
whether we have heard correctly. But before we question it,
let us listen to the experience of another Christian, the apostle Paul. He does not want to boast of his experiences but the
Corinthians have forced him to do so. He then tells of the
visions and revelations he had when fourteen years earlier
he had been taken up into heaven. "Don't ask me whether
my body was there or just my spirit, for I don't know; only
God can answer that. But anyway, there I was in paradise,
and heard things so astounding that they are beyond a man's
power to describe or put in words (and anyway I am not
allowed to tell them to others)" (2 Corinthians 12:2-4).

We can compare this experience with that of Ezekiel,
who said, "Then the Spirit lifted me up and the glory of the
Lord began to move away, accompanied by the sound of a
great earthquake. It was the noise of the wings of the living
beings as they touched against each other, and the sound of
their wheels beside them" (Ezekiel 32:12, 13). After that the
Spirit carried Ezekiel away to Tel Abib beside the Chebar
River.

Again this is similar to what the apostle John saw and
experienced while he was an exile on the island of Patmos.
He had seen a magnificent vision of the glorified Son of Man

among the churches. As he looked he saw a door open in heaven and the voice, like a trumpet blast, of the same Christ invited him to come up there and he would show him what was to happen in the future. Then he said, "Instantly I was, in spirit, there in heaven and saw—oh, the glory of it!—a throne and someone sitting on it! Great bursts of light flashed forth from him as from a glittering diamond, or from a shining ruby, and a rainbow glowing like an emerald encircled his throne" (Revelation 4:2, 3). What glorious sights and experiences! But when all of these great men wrote of them, they presented them as being just as valid as all the other things of which they wrote.

Let us now look at the more common ways that God communicated with man. We will consider God's communication with two outstanding men of the Bible—Abraham of the Old Testament and Paul of the New Testament. Both of these men were changed from ordinary to extraordinary men by learning to listen to and obey the voice of God.

First, God spoke to Abraham by a voice. We do not know how Abraham heard the voice, but it was clear enough that he left his home and family and possessions to obey it. When his nephew was taken as a prisoner by the native peoples and Abraham rescued him, God spoke to him through a priest, giving him great promises. Abraham took it as a message from God, rejecting all spoils from battle, knowing that God would reward him. When he was afraid of those warring people, God spoke to him in a vision, promising him protection from his enemies. As time went by and Abraham became discouraged, God spoke to him in a dream and confirmed the promises and explained them. When later he needed instructions, God twice spoke to him through an angel.

In the same ways, God spoke to Saul, who later became the great apostle Paul, giving him his call through a vision and by a voice, which he obeyed. Besides that, God spoke to him also through prophecy and revelation, as we have seen. But most commonly, God spoke to the apostle by the mysterious and yet common voice of the Holy Spirit.

It is interesting to think about God's speaking to his

people in different languages and by various means. He spoke by voice, by vision, by dream, by prophecy, by angels, by word of wisdom, by word of knowledge, by revelation, and, in earlier times, by the Urim and Thummim and by the lot. We cannot limit the ways of God even to this list, for certainly he spoke to men through daily events, through the word of people, through circumstances, and in ways unknown and often surprising to us. It is hard even to categorize a way by which he spoke in a specific instance. Throughout Scriptures we find that he spoke by his Holy Spirit and yet sometimes he did so through a word of prophecy or a vision or a dream. However, let us look more carefully at specific ways in which God spoke to men.

The most common reference to God's speaking is through what is called the voice of God. Scripture tells of hundreds of times when a voice spoke. Most commonly it is either the voice of a human person or the voice of God. Both are spoken of in the same way. We can say that there must be some similarity. God must speak as man does. Does this mean that the voice of God is audible? That may depend upon the form of God and the form of man. Man is made in the image of God. That does not mean that man is like God physically, but that he is like God in soul and spirit. So, while God speaks as man does, it does not mean that the voice has to be physically audible. God is spirit; he speaks to man by his Spirit. Later we'll see how it is that the spirit of man hears that voice. But we do know that God speaks in such a way that man can understand. When the Bible tells of a man who hears the voice of God, it usually implies God's using some kind of language that the man can understand. There is really communication and conversation between God and man.

Listen to this firsthand report of a conversation between God and one of his prophets:

> *The Lord said to me, "I knew you before you were formed within your mother's womb; before you were born I sanctified you and appointed you as my spokesman to the world." "O Lord God," I said, "I can't do that! I'm*

> *far too young! I'm only a youth!" "Don't say that," he*
> *replied, "for you will go wherever I send you and speak*
> *whatever I tell you to. And don't be afraid of the people,*
> *for I, the Lord, will be with you and see you through"*
> *(Jeremiah 1:4-8).*

This was as natural as a conversation between a father and his son. Furthermore, it was the beginning of free communication between God and Jeremiah that lasted a lifetime. So while we question whether a man can really hear God, these men heard him so clearly that they became messengers of God to the nations. The voice of God became familiar to the prophets. They recognized it and obeyed it.

But even friends looked with suspicion upon those who claimed to hear from God, just as they do today. Aaron and Miriam, the brother and sister of Moses, complained about Moses' wife, but they used the occasion also to question the validity of their brother's ability to hear from God, and they said, "Has the Lord spoken only through Moses? Hasn't he spoken through us too?" The Lord heard them and he called Moses and Aaron and Miriam to the Tabernacle. "Come here, you three," he commanded. Then the Lord descended in the Cloud and stood at the entrance to the Tabernacle, and the voice of the Lord spoke again. "Aaron and Miriam, step forward." When they did, the Lord said to them, "Even with a prophet I would communicate by visions and dreams; but that is not how I communicate with my servant Moses. He is completely at home in my house! With him I speak face to face! And he shall see the very form of God! Why then were you not afraid to criticize him?" (Numbers 12:2-8).

In that very real conversation between God and Moses and his brother and sister we see a form of communication that we have taken for granted as part of the Scriptures. However, if we try to relive that scene in our imagination it raises some interesting questions. For instance, what kind of voice did Aaron and Miriam hear when the Lord called them to appear before him? What did they see when they stood before God? When the Lord descended in the Cloud, was there a special presence of the Lord in the cloud? The whole scene seems more appropriate to an army, where an officer is called before his general, than to a mystical experience of a prophet and his family with God.

God said that he spoke to Moses face to face as a man talks to his friend. They had had an unusually close communication with each other. The more common way that God spoke to the prophets was through dreams and visions—a way that we need to understand better in this day.

The voice of the Lord is not only heard; it is also seen. One of the prophets begins his record with "the burden which Habakkuk, the prophet, did see" (Habakkuk 1:1 KJV) God asked Jeremiah, "What did you see?" (Jeremiah 1:11), and as Jeremiah answers, God gives him the message for Israel. Ezekiel says, "As I was among the captives by the river of Chebar, the heavens were opened and I saw visions of God" (Ezekiel 1:1). So the voice of the Lord is seen through the vision. This is particularly true of the prophets.

The vision shows a reality that cannot be seen with the natural eye. Often it is for encouragement, as it was with Abraham. An encouragement of this kind came to a member of a church where I was pastor. This very fine Christian woman was in great sorrow. Once when she was sitting at her sewing machine weeping, she suddenly sensed a presence at her side. She looked up and sensed that she saw the face of Jesus. It was beautiful beyond description, filled with such comfort and love. A year later she could not even speak of it without tears of joy. It was as if God was saying, "I know that she loves me and talks to me and reads my Word daily, but now she is overwhelmed. She cannot grasp my love by words alone. I will show it to her." And that is what God did through the vision.

Sometimes God shows himself in that way to give comfort. At other times he does it to show a terrible reality. Another believer describes such an experience:

*As evening came and I sat in a darkened room, my
Lord appeared by my side. As I asked, "Lord, is it
You?" the answer came, "I AM." I could but go to
my face on the floor before Him. My eyes flooded with
tears, aware as I was of my own inadequacy and His
overpowering love.*

*Later that night as I lay in bed recalling the sweet-
ness of my day, a vision appeared in the door that almost
frightened me. For a moment I thought it was an emis-
sary of the enemy. Yet deep inside I knew that it was
Christ, as I had never seen Him before. I had seen Him
in majestic splendor with purple robe and golden crown
hallowed in brightness. Often I had seen my Lord in
gentle, white robes as He came to me earlier in the evening. Hand in hand I had run with Him through flow-
ering fields or walked arm in arm by a quiet stream. I
had laid my tear-stained face upon His bosom and
poured out my grief. I had laughed with Him just for the
joy of His presence.*

*But this Christ I saw before me now sent a shudder
through my soul. The tunic He wore came almost to His
knees and the sleeves were large and flowed to His el-
bows. The muscles of His arms and legs were huge and
pronounced and His flesh was as burning brass fresh
from a furnace. In His hand was a weapon similar to a
spear. His eyes were the energy of light: bright and
steady, yet not still, for the energy of that light was in
motion within itself. And as He opened His mouth, His
tongue lashed out like an adder's—broad and forked,
capable of reaching far beyond Himself. The only thing
that kept me from total collapse was the knowledge of the
love between us. I knew this, my precious Lord, would
never bring me hurt. Yet still I watched aghast as the
vision moved toward me and super-imposed itself in my
being. Then the Holy Spirit of the living God spoke.
"This is what the enemy sees, when he looks upon Christ.
Is it any wonder that the demons tremble with fear? And
this is what they see in you, my child, when you take*

authority in the Name of Jesus Christ. What can stand
in the face of My fierceness and why have you fear when
the Lord is on your side?"

The vision, thus, shows reality—whether for encouragement or for instruction or for warning. Visions were so important to the prophets that the Lord once said: "Son of dust, prophesy against the false prophets of Israel who are inventing their own visions and claiming to have messages from me when I have never told them anything at all. Woe upon them!" (Ezekiel 13:2, 3).

Visions were important not only in the Old Testament but also in the New. By visions Zacharias the priest saw the angel of the Lord standing on the right side of the altar of incense. The angel had a wonderful message for him. But because he did not believe it, he was made mute until the child was born. By visions the angels appeared to a group of women and told them of Jesus' resurrection (Luke 24:23). Saul, the persecuter of the Christians, became a believer through a vision. This vision of Christ was so real to him that later he said he had seen Jesus as the disciples did, even though the vision was long after Jesus had died, risen, and ascended into heaven. Furthermore, Paul said he was not disobedient to that heavenly vision. Later he was called to Europe through another vision. We have already seen that John, the much-loved disciple of Jesus, while in exile on the Isle of Patmos for his faith, had a whole series of visions which told about the future.

In many parts of Scripture we have seen that visions were real means by which God communicated with humans. They are a language by which God spoke and apparently still speaks to man. Through visions man can see the word of the Lord as well as hear it. In a similar way God may speak to man through dreams. Dreams and visions are of a similar nature. The Bible is filled with illustrations of God's guidance through dreams and visions. Many important events of the Scriptures hinge upon the message given through one of these means of communication. I was amazed by what I found when I checked every reference to dreams and visions in an exhaustive concordance. In addition to all the external Scripture events which hinge on dreams and visions, I checked all the Bible prophecies which issue out of dreams and visions. I found that the sum of all this material was about equal to the volume of the whole New Testament. This, of course, does not mean that it is equal in value. However, if so much of the Scripture record is occupied with dreams and visions, it must be an important means of communication between God and man.

Just as God used a dream to instruct Pharaoh concerning the future (and so saved his nation and the nation of Israel), so he revealed the thoughts of Nebuchadnezzar's proud heart and caused him to bow before God. Daniel tells us that the dream reveals the thoughts of man's heart. It also reveals what will happen if he continues in the direction he is going (Daniel 2:29, 30).

When a modern man in a dream saw his leg badly swollen so that the red veins stood out like danger signals, he knew that his walk was very badly infected. And when he saw a poisonous spider on his briefcase, he knew that his business or profession would be endangered, too. His own heart was revealed. Another man saw himself climbing a mountain trail with a high mountain on one side and a canyon on the other. His family was following him. As he proceeded up the mountain, the trail became narrower and narrower until it began to crumble under his feet as he awakened. The dream revealed the thoughts of his heart—that which he really knew but was consciously denying. It also showed that he was heading for a fall if he continued in the way he was going at that time. So certain dreams may reveal the thoughts of the heart and show what will happen if we continue to go in the direction we are going.

Abram received the great promises of God for his people through a dream. Jacob was encouraged by his dream to remember God's promises. Joseph was able to save his nation because he could interpret Pharaoh's dream. And Daniel, like Joseph, played a national role through the interpretation of dreams. The Lord appeared to Solomon the great king of Israel in a dream in which he told him to ask for anything he wanted and it would be given to him. Still in the dream Solomon asked for wisdom and God replied that he was pleased with Solomon's request. He gave him wisdom plus riches and honor. When Solomon awakened he realized it had been a dream, and he so definitely believed that God had spoke through the dream that he went to the temple and made his thank-offering to God (1 Kings 3:5-15).

In the New Testament it is the same. In the first chapter we find Joseph with a dream and a very difficult problem. One dream persuaded him that his fiancée was telling the truth, and he believed that God had performed a tremendous miracle by having caused a virgin to conceive. Following that, Joseph received specific directions in a dream, to move his family quickly to Egypt and to return when it was safe again. The dream even indicated where they should live. The wise men also were warned by a dream. So was Pilate's wife.

We may think that God ceased to speak through dreams after the Holy Spirit came, but we should remember that after Jesus' resurrection Peter quoted the prophet Joel saying, " 'In the last days,' God said, 'I will pour out my Holy Spirit upon all mankind, and your sons and daughters shall prophesy, and your old men dream dreams' " (Acts 2:17). The Holy Spirit seems to awaken this very gift for further use. In fact, the Bible has so much to say about this strange language that I shall devote another chapter on the subject of how God speaks through dreams and visions.

Another way God frequently spoke to his people was through prophecy. Prophecy was a message God gave to the prophet to deliver to another person or to a group of people or to a nation. The people receiving the message were getting it indirectly through the prophet. Those giving prophecy received their messages directly from God through a word in their own language or through a vision or a dream.

A particular principle was involved in prophecy. (See Jeremiah 18:1-10.) God's judgment through the prophet did not necessarily take place as predicted. The prophecy was a warning. If the people or nation to whom the prophecy was given did not repent, the judgment came upon them. But if they repented they were spared. Thus, when Jonah declared that Nineveh would be destroyed in forty days, and we find that it was not destroyed, we know that it was all in keeping with the principle of prophecy, for the people of the city repented. Similarly, if a prophet gave a promise from God, that promise would not be fulfilled of itself, but only if the person continued in the positive way he was going. If not, the prophecy would not be fulfilled. Other laws concerning the prophet and prophecy will be taken up later.

Prophecy takes up a good portion of the Old Testament, and the prophets occupied a very important place in the sight of God. In the New Testament, prophethood is bestowed upon John the Baptist and fulfilled in Jesus. The line of prophets does not end even in Jesus. As Paul shows in his letter to Ephesus, prophecy still has a place in the New Testament church as a gift from the risen Lord. "And he gave some, apostles; and some, prophets; and some, evangelists; and some, pastors and teachers" (Ephesians 4:11 KJV). We also see the gift of prophecy exercised by the apostles in such events as those recorded in the book of Acts, and especially by John, as recorded in the book of Revelation.

This gift of prophecy, almost lost in the modern church, is finding an awakening today. Like other gifts, the gift of prophecy must be recognized, tested, and proved. The gift of prophecy takes a different approach in the New Testament than in the Old. In the Old Testament we often find the prophet saying, "Thus says the Lord." In the New Testament the prophet speaks with the Spirit within him. Often his word may seem like a casual word, but the one to whom it is spoken can recognize it as the word of God for himself. It has the power of the Spirit to verify its truth.

It was a surprise to my wife, Lillie, and me when a group of reliable Christian pastors and elders gave us a word that we would be going to many lands beside many waters. As it was prophesied we were told that we would be given a message and with it all opposition would be overcome in all places where he sent us. It was told to us quietly and we were asked whether our hearts confirmed it. This proved to be a word remarkably fulfilled as we traveled in more than thirty countries to visit Protestant missionaries and lay-people, Catholic priests and nuns, university professors and African pastors, doctors and psychiatrists and counselors and people of all walks of life. We had only to be careful to obey the principle of prophecy which says that if we continue to trust and obey God, this promise would be fulfilled. For eight years it has been true for us. Prophecy has become a relevant word from God for our circumstances.

The Holy Spirit also spoke through the word of wisdom and knowledge. The apostle Paul in his letter to the Corinthians (1 Corinthians 12—14) mentions the manifestations of the Holy Spirit through gifts of men. We see these gifts at work in the church of the book of Acts. Among them are the word of wisdom and the word of knowledge. Evidently the Spirit of God gave to Stephen the word of wisdom when he was challenged in an argument by men of several countries. He was not prepared to meet this challenge. But as Jesus had said, "When you are arrested, don't worry about what to say at your trial, for you will be given the right words at the right time. For it won't be you doing the talking—it will be the Spirit of your heavenly Father speaking through you!" (Matthew 10:19, 20). Luke, the writer of the book of Acts, tells us that when Stephen spoke out with wisdom, the formidable opposition was not able to stand against Stephen's wisdom (Acts 6). In a similar way, the word of wisdom may come to a mother when she cannot answer her rebellious son. Or to a man who is seeking to be a witness in his business. When we are in a test and our wisdom runs out, God has a special wisdom which he may give as a gift for the occasion.

In a similar way, we see the gift of knowledge at work in the apostle Peter's life (Acts 5). In the midst of a sharing meeting, a man said that he and his wife had sold some land and brought all the money from it to the church. Evidently at that moment, the Spirit of God revealed to Peter that the couple had kept back part of the money and so were lying. They did not have to bring any of the money, but they did need to tell the truth. In separate confrontations he challenged the man and his wife. When they did not repent, they both suddenly fell dead. That was clear evidence that Peter was not speaking from himself, but was guided by the Spirit of God. Thus, the gift of knowledge, as well as wisdom, is a manifestation of the Holy Spirit given, as Jesus said, for power to witness to Christ.

A woman asked me to pray for her and told me what her need was. But while I prayed, the Holy Spirit was telling me to mention another matter. I did not want to mention it but the Lord was insistent, so I finally did mention it in my prayer for God's healing. As soon as I was through praying, the woman looked up and said, "You must have been led of God, for you mentioned my *real* need, which I did not want to tell you about." Often the word of knowledge is not recognized by the one who gives it but by the one who receives it, as he stands amazed that his heart has been revealed. This is the way it was when Jesus suddenly by a word of knowledge revealed the hidden life of the woman at the well of Samaria (John 4). Amazed, she went home and spoke of Jesus as a prophet, telling the people of her village, "Come and meet a man who told me everything I ever did. Can this be the Messiah?" (John 4:29).

As if all these ways of God's speaking were not enough, we find that in particular times of need God also sends angels to be the messengers of his word. Most of us have never seen an angel, but the Scripture says, "The angels are only spiritual messengers sent out to help and care for those who are to receive his salvation" (Hebrews 1:14). That is what they have been to man.

One day two angels appearing like men came to Abraham and Sarah to tell them about the son who had been promised and for whom they had been waiting twenty-five years. Some years later God sent his angel again, this time to call out from the sky, keeping Abraham from literally making an offering of his son. What wonderful messengers they were! The angels even came to Lot in that wicked city of Sodom to spare him and his family, literally taking him and his wife by the hands and dragging them out of the city.

H. A. Baker, in his book *Heaven and the Angels,*[5] tells of an American man in China who could speak Japanese as well as Chinese.

> *In conversation with men of the Japanese Air Force, he was told that one of their airmen was dispatched to lead a number of planes in attacking a Chinese town. When nearing the town, his own plane leading, he suddenly saw a white cloud appear in the distance. As his plane neared the cloud, he saw a group of angels. His plane became unsteady. Repeatedly he endeavored to direct his plane in the direction of the town but the hindering cloud of angels made it so impossible to control his plane that he circled around and, followed by the others, returned to the base from which he started. Since he did not attack the town and the Japanese authorities did not believe in angels, the leader of this attacking plane was executed for disobedience.*
>
> *The American who related this also got the other side of the story. In that town to be attacked great apprehension was felt because of the impending danger, as an attack from airplanes was hourly expected. In that place was a little group of Chinese Christians led by a consecrated old Chinese pastor. In view of this imminent danger, the pastor and his people gave themselves to praying to the God of Daniel. On the day of the attack, the pastor was praying to Him who said He would give the angels charge over His people. The people in the town did not see the angels, but they saw the airplane in the lead circle around and return with the other planes following.*

This is like the experiences of God's protection for his people as recorded in the Scriptures.

In the New Testament record, we have already found how the angel came to Zacharias, the father of John the Baptist, through a vision. We find also that the same great angel came to tell the virgin Mary that she was to be the mother of the Son of God. This news was so great that a whole host of angels appeared to the shepherds with the good news. Later on Jesus was strengthened by an angel when he was wrestling for us in prayer. It seems that God sent his angels to carry out his word at strategic times. An angel came and opened the jail for Peter as the church was praying. Paul was encouraged by an angel when he and his shipmates were undergoing shipwreck. It seems that these messengers of God appeared at special times of need, ready to help, strengthen, protect, and encourage God's people.

A friend from India suggests that the reason why we in America so seldom see or receive the help of angels is that we seldom venture beyond our ability to take care of ourselves. If we need something for which we don't have money, we simply use a credit card. If we need protection, we call the police. Those who do not have access to such help, but do trust in God, will receive supernatural help.

These are all ways by which God spoke to man, some more frequently than others. But there was also a time when God led Israel by the means of the *Urim* and *Thummim*—something the priests carried, which produced oracular responses. Both David and Solomon got messages from God by this means. But later the prophets replaced the Urim and Thummim.

Another means of seeking guidance occasionally was the *lot,* such as the apostles used as late as the week before Pentecost, when Matthias was chosen to take the place of Judas. Scripture says little about either of these last two ways of obtaining God's guidance. The marvelous thing is that God does not content himself to speak to us in only one way. If we do not hear him, he speaks in another and yet another way.

We do not know how Job heard God speak but we do know that Elihu, the last of the friends to speak to Job, said, "My heart trembles at this. Listen, listen to the thunder of his voice. It rolls across the heavens and his lightning flashes out in every direction. Afterwards comes the roaring of the thunder—the tremendous voice of his majesty. His voice is glorious in the thunder. We cannot comprehend the greatness of his power" (Job 37:1-5).

After that, the Lord answered Job from the whirlwind or hurricane. It may well be that a frightening storm passed over them, shaking them to their depths, so that afterwards thoughts began to rush in upon Job, and he heard God saying, "Why are you using your ignorance to deny my providence? Now get ready to fight, for I am going to demand some answers from you, and you must reply. Where were you when I laid the foundation of the earth?" Then came another challenge, "Do you still want to argue with the Almighty? Or will you yield? Do you—God's critic—have the answers?" Then Job (perhaps only in his heart) answered God: "I am nothing—how could I ever find the answers? I lay my hand upon my mouth in silence." And as God's thoughts continued to come upon him, Job's heart responded to God. Job said, "I know that you can do anything and that no one can stop you. You ask who it is who has so foolishly denied your providence. It is I. I was talking about things I knew nothing about, and did not understand, things far too wonderful for me." Then Job seemed to come to a new understanding through a two-dimensional look at God. "I had heard about you before, but now I have seen you, and I loathe myself and repent in dust and ashes." (See Job 42:2-5.)

In the terror of the storm, God may have spoken to the three friends, in the same way, causing them to repent and seek the prayer of Job—after which God restored Job to a position even greater than he had before. It may be that many years later God revealed to Job the source of all his troubles. We do not know whether that was the way it all came about, but we do know that God uses many means and many languages to speak to us—sometimes to warn us, sometimes to encourage, sometimes to challenge us. It is for us to learn to understand the languages in which he speaks.

5
How God Speaks through the Scriptures

It was early in the summer of 1970 in Zurich, Switzerland. Lillie and I had in hand invitations from missionaries in ten countries asking us to come and minister to them. When I asked them about the dates that they would like us to come, they suggested that I set up the schedule the way that suited us. But how could I arrange a schedule to speak to groups of missionaries who are often away from their homes in the tribal areas for months at a time? It would be impossible to arrive at the right time in all of those places in ten countries around the world. At least so it seemed to me.

But I had the invitations and the Lord had said that we should go. So I went to the BOAC airlines office in Zurich and told the ticket agent that I wanted to arrange a three month round-the-world trip to Lahore, Kathmandu, Bangkok, Saigon, Hongkong, Fujinomiya, Manila, Port Moresby, Darwin, Brisbane, Sydney, Melbourne, Christchurch, and Auckland. While I was puzzling about the schedule, a promise of Scripture which the Lord had given me earlier, kept repeating itself to me. "I will go before thee, and make the crooked places straight" (Isaiah 45:2 KJV). That phrase kept going through my mind almost like a ringing in my ears. But in two hours the agent and I set up a round-the-world tour including all the cities I had asked about.

The trip lasted ten and one-half months instead of the three months I had anticipated. But that is where I first learned by experience how wonderfully the Lord arranges schedules if we will cooperate with him. It was amazing to see how beautifully that schedule worked out. Over and over again it proved to be just the right time to arrive. When there was a cancellation of an invitation which meant that we had two weeks with no schedule and little money on the other side of the world, the Lord's timing was still right. A medical doctor had been at a dinner party with us in the brief stop in Bangkok. When he later learned of the cancellation he brought us back on a 3,000-mile detour to minister for two weeks to sixty missionaries he felt should hear the lectures.

On another occasion we arrived at the mission base the very day that the annual speaker had left. That meant that many of the missionaries who had gathered for the annual conference were now scattering to their tribal locations many miles apart. However that, too, proved to be the right timing. We learned that, by his messages, the former speaker had prepared the way for our coming. Furthermore, we were staying longer in this place than in any other, so we had the joy of entering into another's work and carrying it on to the harvest. This was evidently the Lord's doing. He went before us and made the crooked places straight—in fact, much "straighter" than if we had known about the missionaries' schedules and made the "proper" plans accordingly.

Thus a promise in the Scriptures was the voice of God to me. And there are many other ways that God speaks through the Scriptures. Often he speaks through the examples—good or bad—of the men and women of the Bible. We are encouraged to believe God as Abel, Enoch, Noah, Abraham, Sarah, and others did. But where an example is not good, we are to take a lesson from their unbelief. The apostle Paul said:

> *We must never forget, dear brothers, what happened to our people in the wilderness long ago. God guided them by sending a cloud that moved along ahead of them; and he brought them all safely through the waters of the Red Sea—Yet after all this, most of them did not obey God, and he destroyed them in the wilderness. From this lesson we are warned that we must not desire evil things as they did, nor worship idols as they did. Another lesson for us is what happened when some of them sinned with other men's wives, and 23,000 fell dead in one day. All these things happened to them as examples, as object lessons to us, to warn us against doing the same things; they were written down so that we could read about them and learn from them in these last days as the world nears its end. (1 Corinthians 10:1-13)*

God may also speak to us through the great principles of faith we find in God's dealing with men over the generations. Solomon gathered together a book of proverbs such as the saying, "The good man walks along in the ever-brightening light of God's favor; the dawn gives way to morning splendor, while the evil man gropes and stumbles in the dark" (Proverbs 4:18, 19). Another basic principle is found in his saying, "For the reverence and fear of God are basic to all wisdom. Knowledge of God results in every other kind of understanding" (Proverbs 9:10). Illustrated throughout the rest of the Bible is the truth, "Godliness exalts a nation, but sin is a reproach to any people" (Proverbs 14:34).

Then the Lord may call us to enter into songs of praise and worship with the psalmist. "I will praise the Lord no matter what happens. I will constantly speak of his glories and grace. I will boast of all his kindness to me. Let all who are discouraged take heart. Let us praise the Lord together, and exalt his name" (Psalm 34:1-3). This is not to be done lightly but in the spirit of the psalmist who said, "I bless the Holy Name of God with all my heart." In praising God not only our hearts but our minds are to be included. "...and not forget the glorious things he does for me" (Psalm 103:1, 2). If we listen we hear him call every *thing* ("Sun and moon, and all you twinkling stars") and every*one* ("Let everything alive give praises to the Lord! You praise him! Hallelujah!") (Psalms 148:3 and 150:6). In the praises to God we hear him speak.

The New Testament is filled with direct teaching for to-day. In the rich instruction of the Sermon on the Mount and in his wayside teachings, Jesus speaks to all of us. And in the parables Jesus speaks to all who will *hear,* while the rest fail to understand.

Jesus had given a promise that the Holy Spirit would teach us and guide us into all truth. In a critical spirit we can take quotations from the Bible and make them "prove" many contradictory things. But this cannot be so if the Spirit of God is guiding us. The Holy Spirit leads our thoughts in lines with the thoughts of the real author, who is God himself. Paul, speaking of God's hidden wisdom that is far beyond the understanding of this world, says, "Things beyond our seeing, things beyond our hearing, things beyond our imagining, all prepared by God for those who love him—these it is that God has revealed to us through the Spirit." Then, comparing our understanding of men, he goes on to say, "Among men, who knows what a man is but the man's own spirit within him? In the same way, only the Spirit of God knows what God is. This is the Spirit that we have received from God" (1 Corinthians 2:9-12 NEB).

It is the Spirit of God who makes the Scriptures live. It is he who has guided the Bible writers in recording events and it is he who makes those experiences alive to us. We hear it said that as one is reading the Scriptures suddenly a verse or phrase seems to rise right out of the page. It is the Spirit of God who takes a word and applies it to our hearts for the occasion.

For instance, through the Law God had long ago said

that if Israel would not listen and obey his commandments, "the heavens above you will be as unyielding as bronze, and the earth beneath will be as iron. The land will become as dry as dust for lack of rain, and dust storms shall destroy you" (Deuteronomy 28:23, 24). That warning had been a part of the Law for many generations and it had lain there. But one day a man by the name of Elijah became deeply disturbed about Israel's sin. The apostle James says that he prayed much. Then the Spirit of God took the old warning and made it to live in Elijah's heart and he spoke to the king of Israel, saying, "As surely as the Lord God of Israel lives— the God whom I worship and serve—there won't be any dew or rain for several years until I say the word!" (1 Kings 17:1). It did not rain for three and a half years. Then Elijah prayed and it rained again. Without the Spirit, the word of the Law had produced no fruit. But the Spirit brought it to life. Elijah, the prophet, was the instrument to carry the voice of God. Yet James tells us, "Elijah was as completely human as we are, and yet when he prayed earnestly that no rain would fall, none fell for the next three and one half years! Then he prayed again, this time that it would rain, and down it poured and the grass turned green and the gardens began to grow again" (James 5:17, 18). Thus God speaks through the Scriptures when the Spirit of God makes them alive.

Likewise the Spirit of God also gives understanding of the meaning of the Scriptures. For instance, Jesus said, "Do not imagine that I have come to abolish, but to complete them. You have learned how it was said to our ancestors: You must not kill; and if anyone does kill, he must answer for it before the court." Then, five times over, Jesus says, "But I say this to you"—lifting the law from its literal interpretation to the Spirit of it. (See Matthew 5.) So Jesus shows by the Spirit that there is a deeper meaning in the Law.

The apostle Paul does the same thing. He refers to the law that forbade the Israelite to muzzle an ox to keep it from eating while it was treading out the wheat. Then he points out the deeper meaning. "Do you suppose God was thinking only about oxen when he said this? Wasn't he also thinking

about us? Of course he was. He said this to show us that
Christian workers should be paid by those they help. Those
who do the plowing and threshing should expect some share
of the harvest" (1 Corinthians 9:1, 10).

God indeed speaks to us through the Scriptures, but he
does so by his Spirit and not simply by the record of the
things that are written there. We have seen serious teaching
of the Scriptures, and even memorizing of it, without the
Spirit's power; and we have seen it die without bearing fruit.
But "We are free to serve God, not in the old obedience to
the letter of the law, but in the new way, in the Spirit" (Romans 7:6). For it is the Spirit of God who interprets these
records, and beyond the records themselves we see Christ.
In light of that, Paul, speaking of Israel's experience in the
days of Moses, said, "And did all eat the same spiritual meat;
and did all drink the same spiritual drink: for they drank of
that spiritual Rock that followed them; and that Rock was
Christ" (1 Corinthians 10:3, 4 KJV). Even in meditation upon
the Scriptures, Christ himself becomes our spiritual food.

For this reason C. S. Lewis said:

> *The Scriptures proceed not by conversion of God's word
> into a literature but by taking up of a literature to be a
> vehicle of God's word. Just in the same way, Scripture
> can be read as merely human literature. One who con-
> tended that a poem was nothing but black marks on
> white paper would be unanswerable if he addressed an
> audience who couldn't read. Look at it through micro-
> scopes, analyze the printer's ink and the paper, study it
> (in that way) as long as you like; you will never find
> something over and above all the products of analysis
> whereof you can say, "This is a poem." Those who can
> read, however, will continue to say the poem exists. If the
> Old Testament is a literature thus "taken up," made the
> vehicle of what is more than human, we can hardly set
> any limit to the weight or multiplicity of meanings which
> may have been laid upon it.*[6]

It is the Spirit of God who thus takes up the literature of
the Bible itself and through it reveals to us the mysteries of

God and leads us into fellowship with our Lord Jesus. There-fore, it is important that we get acquainted with all the Scriptures. If there are portions that we have not read, how can God speak to us through those portions? Some parts may be dull indeed, and do not seem to have any application to us at all until the Spirit of God applies them to our circumstances.

This also demands a full yieldedness of our whole selves to God. Jesus, answering a question about which is the most important commandment, says, "The one that says, 'Hear, O Israel! The Lord our God is the one and only God. And you must love him with all your heart and soul and mind and strength'" (Mark 12:29, 30). If we love God with all our heart and soul and mind and strength then we will also love to hear what he has to say to us. Our minds have been so influenced by the lives of the enemy and by the half truths of the world and by the limitations of our traditions, that it is hard for us to hear the whole truth of what God is saying. By study of the Scriptures and meditation upon them, our minds become enlightened and we see truth in a new light. We are set free. But to experience this we must come to God with an open mind.

To hear him aright, we need to yield to God our whole soul, including our emotions. How frequently we are called upon to praise God with our whole beings. "Shout with joy before the Lord, O earth! Obey him gladly; come before him, singing with joy!" (Psalm 100:1, 2). This is a reminder of what we need in our churches. Sometimes we offer our minds to God in the acceptance of doctrine or theology but give our emotions to the football game or the soap opera. If we are going to hear God properly, our emotions must also enter in. They must neither be stifled nor allowed to run wild, but must join with the heart and mind in reading the Bible. How barren Scriptures become when we don't let our feelings enter into the experience of the writers!

On the other hand, what insights come in the midst of true worship of God! King Jehoshaphat received a great victory because he believed the message of the prophet and did a militarily preposterous thing. Who ever heard of a choir going ahead of a military unit in battle? But the proph-et had said that they were to believe in God for success, and

Jehoshaphat demonstrated his faith in God rather than in his sword, by putting the choir ahead of the swords. This is what happened:

> *After consultation with the leaders of the people, he determined that there should be a choir leading the march, clothed in sanctified garments and singing the song, 'His lovingkindness is forever' as they walked along praising and thanking the Lord. And at the moment they began to sing and to praise, the Lord caused the armies of Ammon, Moab, and Mount Seir to begin fighting among themselves, and they destroyed each other! (2 Chronicles 20:21, 22)*

There must also be that quiet time with God in order to hear him speak. The staretz of Russia spent much time alone, often wandering through forests listening to God, and in that way received the voice of God. At the Madonna House in Combermere, Ontario, it is expected that every member of the order will spend a full 24-hour day in the "Postinia," a house in the woods furnished only with a Bible, a pitcher of water, a loaf of bread, a cot, a table, and a chair, that they may listen and hear God speak. All the great saints of God have done similar things. The same Spirit who directed the prophets and the men of God, wants to direct us in similar ways if we will take time to listen to him—not only to read the word of God, but to meditate upon it.

Too often we hasten through our readings without hearing the Lord speak. I have found it very worthwhile going through a gospel, or an epistle or the Psalms, to take just one or two, at most three verses at a time and meditate upon them in depth until I received a message from the Lord. There is no way in this age of minute meals and jet travel to substitute a hurried devotional time for the quietness that is demanded if we are going to communicate to God. My good friend and professor, Dr. B. B. Sutcliffe, used to say, "If you take an hour for your quiet time and it takes you fifty minutes 'to shut the door,' it is better to have ten minutes of quietness with God, than spend an hour in which you have never closed the door on the outside world and on any plaguing inward thoughts, so that you can really hear the Lord."

When we are meditating upon the Scriptures, we are letting the experiences of the believers from many centuries filter through our minds and hearts to correct us with their laws, inspire us with their songs, challenge us with their prophecies, and speak personally to us with their letters. We will later look to see how we need to know not only the Bible records, but the principles that are involved therein, to test our experiences with them. We will see how important it is that we check all that we hear with the guidelines given in the Scriptures; for as God has spoken with men of the past, he speaks in the same way to us and he does not contradict himself.

6
How God Speaks through Dreams and Visions

Let us now look more closely at another language in which God speaks to man. Dreams and visions are part of the elementary language of God—the language of pictures and symbols, sometimes referred to as "dark speeches" or "riddles."

We will remember that one day as the brother and sister of Moses questioned his ability to hear God more clearly than they could hear him, God called the three of them to task. "And he said, Hear now my words; if there be a prophet among you, I the Lord will make myself known unto him in a vision, and will speak unto him in a dream" (Numbers 12:6 KJV). Or as other translations put it, "I speak with him face to face, plainly and not in riddles" (JB) or "plainly, not obscurely" (verse 8, BV).

We may well wonder why God should speak obscurely or in riddles. Why does he not speak plainly so that we can all understand? We get a clue to the answer to this question from Jesus. The disciples found the parables hard to understand, and Matthew tells us,

> *"His disciples came and asked him, 'Why do you always use these hard to understand illustrations?' Then he explained to them that only they were permitted to understand about the Kingdom of Heaven, and others were not. 'For to him who has will more be given,' he told them, 'and he will have great plenty; but from him who has not, even the little he has will be taken away. This is why I use these illustrations, so people will hear and see but not understand.' " (Matthew 13:10-13).*

Jesus spoke parables so that those who really wanted to follow him would be able to understand and so that those who were just curious would not find their way. This agrees with the principle he **set forth** in the Beatitudes when he said, "The meek and lowly are fortunate! for they shall be comforted" (Matthew 5:6). The apostle John quoted Jesus saying, "Look! I have been standing at the door and I am constantly knocking. If anyone hears me calling him and opens the door, I will come in and fellowship with him and he with me" (Revelation 3:20). He always waits until he is invited before he comes into a life. "On the last day, the climax of the holidays, Jesus shouted to the crowds, 'If anyone is thirsty, let him come to me and drink' " (John 7:37). God does not give his best gifts to those who have only a casual interest in them. Jesus said, "Ask, and you will be given what you ask for. Seek, and you will find. Knock, and the door will be opened" (Matthew 7:7).

So it is also with the understanding of dreams and visions. Unless we have a real interest in hearing from God, we will not bother to seek to understand our dreams. But if we really want to know and obey him, dreams give us an opportunity to understand ourselves better so that we can find our fulfillment in God. This is only for those whose desire is deep, not superficial. If the miner is willing to make long tunnels into the heart of the earth to find precious ore, and if Thomas Edison was willing to make thousands of experiments before he succeeded in inventing the light bulb, how much more should we be willing to study diligently to learn the language of dreams and visions by which God so often speaks to his people.

What do these dreams or riddles mean? Are they the wishful thinking of men, as some say? Certainly the dreams of the men and women in the Bible were not that. Instead they were like mirrors. A mirror accurately reflects our physical appearance. When we look into it upon our awakening, it is usually not complimentary. So also the dream accurately reflects the condition of our hearts, though often to our shame and embarrassment. But as a mirror reflects the changes we make in our appearance, so the dream reflects the changes that we make in our hearts. This is the lesson that Daniel, the great authority on dreams and visions, has taught us, as we shall later see.

The language of dreams and visions is one which God used often to speak to man. Why, then, have we ignored this language? Because we have been influenced by the Aristotelian philosophy of the Western world that says knowledge can be obtained only through the five senses and reason; all other knowledge is suspect. This philosophy has caused us to disregard great portions of the Scriptures, including the indirect language of God speaking through dreams and visions. However, God's obscure language is still valid. In the book of Job we learn of three ways that God speaks to warn. He speaks to the heart, and then if a person does not listen, "God speaks again and again, in dreams, in visions of the night when deep sleep falls on men as they lie on their beds. He opens their ears in times like that, and gives them wisdom and instruction, causing them to change their minds, and keeping them from pride, and warning them of the penalties of sin, and keeping them from falling into some trap" (Job 33:14-18).

If a man will not listen to the voice of the dream and vision, then "God sends sickness and pain, even though no bone is broken, so that a man loses all taste and appetite for food and doesn't care for even the daintiest dessert. He be-

comes thin, mere skin and bones, and draws near to death"
(Job 33:19-22). We find many in the hospitals today who
have heard God speak to them inwardly but did not obey.
Then God warned them through their dreams and night-
mares, but having been taught not to pay attention to
dreams, or at least having no understanding of them, they
have ignored them. Then the third step, sickness, comes
upon them, either physically or psychologically. This has
been a pattern from the day of Job, a very early writer of the
Bible, and on to the present time.

Daniel, a great biblical authority on dreams and visions,
had suffered a great deal, having been taken captive as a
youth. Perhaps he had seen his parents killed before he was
taken to a strange country. Like Joseph, Daniel had been
prepared through suffering to learn to understand and
interpret dreams. Nebuchadnezzar, on the other hand, as
ruler of the greatest nation on the face of the earth at that
time, thought his will could not be challenged. But God had
another way to speak to such a man.

Daniel records for us the running conversation between
God and Nebuchadnezzar. He shows us the value of understanding the warning and instruction given through dreams.
We will also see how Daniel, a man of God, was able to save
himself and be the instrument to cause Nebuchadnezzar to
humble himself before God. Furthermore, in the night-time
conversation between God and Nebuchadnezzar we can
learn from Daniel some principles to help us understand
dreams and visions (Daniel 1—4).

Because Nebuchadnezzar's heart was too proud to listen
to the quiet voice of God within, God warned him through
dreams. The first recorded dream was a frightening nightmare, because Nebuchadnezzar's condition had become so
serious. He had probably had many other dreams but had
failed to pay attention to them. It is far better to listen to the
message of the gentle nightly dreams and receive correction
than to allow the condition to become so bad that it is reflected in a nightmare.

Nebuchadnezzar could not remember his dreams. That
is a common complaint of people when their attention is

called to the value of the dream message. There are several reasons why we do not remember our dreams. First of all, we have learned to ignore them. Many people begin to remember their dreams when their attention is called to them. Another reason for forgetting our dreams is the alarm clock and especially the radio-alarm that cuts off our sleep in such a way that a buzzer or a radio announcer's voice or a commercial comes rushing in to replace the dream. God's thoughts are delicate, they demand stillness. So do the messages of dreams he sends. We must listen quietly to such a dream and write it down, as Daniel did, before it is pushed away by our thoughts. However, there is another reason why we do not remember our dreams. If we want to shut God out of our thoughts or dreams, we may do so for a while and thus we forget the dream. And evidently this is what Nebuchadnezzar had tried to do. He did not want to listen to God's voice. Finally, however, God broke through, though his condition was then already critical.

Daniel got the dream and its interpretation from God through prayer. At that point he noted two basic principles concerning the message of dreams, as he tells the king, "You, O king, as you lay in bed, were thinking of the future, speculating as to what should come to pass hereafter, and he who reveals secrets disclosed to you what is going to happen. As for myself, this secret has not been revealed to me because of any wisdom I possess more than other men, but in order that the meaning may be known to the king and that you, O king, may understand the thoughts of your own heart" (Daniel 2:29, 30 BJ).

Daniel says Nebuchadnezzar's dreams showed two things in particular. First, the thoughts of his heart over against the thoughts of his mind. Second, what would happen if he would continue in the direction in which he was going. The thoughts of the king's mind were that he was ruler over all men, even to the point of having them worship him. The dream showed him what would happen if he continued to follow the thoughts of his mind only. Like prophecy, dreams (compare Jeremiah 18:1-10) indicated what will happen if we continue in the direction we are going. If we heed the warning and change the direction, the judgment will not fall on us. But if we do not heed the warning, the judgment is sure.

The thoughts of Nebuchadnezzar's mind were that no one was greater than he. So in the first dream he saw a statue whose head was of gold, the shoulders of silver, the belly of brass, the legs of iron, and the feet of iron and clay. Daniel said that the head of gold represented Nebuchadnezzar himself. This indicated that his kingdom was greater than the succeeding ones. But in the dream he also saw a great boulder, cut out of a mountain, that came hurtling down, crushing the statue to powder. That boulder then became the great mountain itself. This told him that there was a greater kingdom than any of those pictured by the statue, and that even his own great kingdom would finally pass away.

However, Nebuchadnezzar did not heed the warning of the dream. Instead, he built his statue all of gold, saying in effect that his kingdom was for all time and that there would be no kingdom to follow. When he then commanded all people to bow before that statue, he demanded worship that belongs only to God. So in his heart, Nebuchadnezzar defied the God who gave him the first dream. When the friends of Daniel stood up to the king and God defended them in the furnace, Nebuchadnezzar acknowledged that there was a great God, "For no other God can do what this one does" (Daniel 3:29). But we see that in his heart Nebuchadnezzar was not yet humbled before God, for the second dream reveals further his heart's condition. Dreams change as we change, and Nebuchadnezzar had changed only outwardly. His heart remained proud.

The second dream warned him further. In it he saw a very tall tree that grew higher and higher until it could be seen by all the earth. (Note: higher than Nebuchadnezzar's 90-foot statue.) All the birds and animals were sheltered in that tree, and it was filled with fruit so that all the earth was fed by it. Then an angel from God commanded that the tree be cut down, its branches be cut off, and the animals and birds permitted to scatter. But the trunk and roots of the tree were to remain. Then the image changed. This tree seemed to become a man and the man received the heart of an animal.

This dream was a terrible warning. Daniel had told him to stop sinning and to do what he knew was right, so that God might spare him. It frightened the king enough so that he paid attention to it for a time. But before a year was over, he forgot the warning. Then, just as the dream had said, so it happened. Notice how accurately the dream was fulfilled because he continued in his proud ways. After twelve months the king, walking in his palace, said, "I, by my own mighty power, have built this beautiful city as my royal residence, and as the capital of my empire." The words had not left his lips before he heard a voice from heaven. "O King Nebuchadnezzar, this message is for you: You are no longer ruler of this kingdom. You will be forced out of the palace to live with the animals in the fields, and to eat grass like the cows for seven years until you finally realize that God parcels out the kingdoms of men and gives them to anyone he chooses" (Daniel 4:30-32).

History tells us that the king lost his mind and was removed from his throne—the tree was cut down. His far-reaching influence over men was lost—the branches were cut off. He was put out to the field as they did in those days to those who had lost their minds. Out there he became wet with the dew of heaven. Though he had lost his mind, his heart was still able to respond to God—the trunk and the roots remained so the tree could grow again (as trees do in warm climates). Then we read, "At the end of seven years, I, Nebuchadnezzar, looked up to heaven, and my sanity returned, and I praised and worshipped the Most High God and honored him who lives forever, whose rule is everlasting, his kingdom evermore. When my mind returned to me, so did my honor and glory and kingdom." He was then reestablished in his throne with greater honor than before. He then showed signs of true repentance towards God from his heart, saying, "Now I, Nebuchadnezzar, praise and glorify and honor the king of Heaven, the Judge of all, whose every act is right and good; for he is able to take those who walk proudly and push them into the dust!" (Daniel 4:34-37).

The frightening conversation between God and Nebuchadnezzar ended when the king finally humbled himself. Such is the kind of conversation God holds with many people, warning them of destruction that is sure to come if they will not change their ways. If they would only listen to their dreams they could avoid great troubles. A dream is not always frightening, of course. Sometimes it is beautiful, comforting, and even promising, as were the dreams of Joseph and Jacob and Solomon.

Visions come from the same source as dreams from the deepest level of the psyche, through which God speaks to man. In the Bible the word *dream* and the word *vision* are sometimes used interchangeably. Dreams, of course, come while we are asleep; visions while awake. A vision shows a reality that cannot be seen with our physical eyes; therefore it is frightening. That is the reason why the first word that the angels say when they appear is, "Do not be afraid." The shepherds of Bethlehem were shocked to see a glorious reality that they did not know was there. So it was with Zacharias, the priest, when Gabriel appeared to him.

As I was traveling in Mexico a few years ago, a friend pointed out a mountain above a little town. He said that a group of Christians were so greatly persecuted in the town, that they decided to build some huts up on the side of the mountain and live there. One evening as the pastor was away, his wife gathered the Christians together for prayer, for they often lived in fear of the townspeople. The next morning as some of the Christians went down to the town below, they were surprised to find the townspeople looking at them in awe. When they inquired, they learned that the night before, while the little Christian group was praying, the men in the town in their hatred had climbed the mountain, determined to burn down the huts of the believers. But on the way they met an army that so frightened them that they turned back. It was not the Mexican Army that they saw. By vision, they saw the reality of the angels of the Lord surrounding his children as they were praying. It was a reality that they had not counted on, but God allowed them to see, to keep them from their purpose. Similar reports of a whole unit of an army seeing the same vision have come from both world wars.

Take note of two principles in regard to dreams and visions in Scripture. First, they were personal. Abram's great dream told of God's oath to him as he received a promise and was waiting anxiously for its fulfillment. Joseph's dream told of the possibility of his prominent position among his brothers—a dream that must have given him great assurance through the long difficult days as a slave and in the dungeon. The butler and the baker whom Joseph met in the prison had dreams that told them of their immediate personal future. Pharaoh dreamed concerning his land of Egypt. God's call to Samuel at night gave him his personal call to become the prophet of God. In Solomon's dream God offered to give him whatever he asked. Daniel's dream concerned the nations, but so did his personal interests. Our dreams are as big as our interests. Joseph, who was engaged to Mary, received his personal answer to the question of his marriage through a dream, and then received detailed instruction concerning his little family's safety and the place of their lodging. So personal were the dreams of the Bible.

The visions too were personal, for encouragement or to strengthen faith. Take for example the appearance of the angel to the frightened women after the resurrection and the personal word of encouragement to Paul at the time of his shipwreck. Even Peter's vision (Acts 10) that led him to accept the believers in Cornelius' house, which opened the way for the first great solution to the problem of integration in the Christian church, was a personal vision. It showed him the prejudice that still existed within his heart. Faced with his prejudice through that vision, Peter allowed God to deal with it. The revelation of Jesus Christ concerning the future was made personally to John. Because John's interest was for the whole church, so was the vision. The personal aspect of dreams and visions will be important to us when we look at laws of interpretation later in this book.

The second principle we see in the dreams and visions of Scripture is that they speak in a language different from the language of the mind. Dreams and visions speak by symbols and images, rather than by reason. Often symbols are not recognized in dreams because they are taken from the everyday circumstances or activities of the dreamer. It was so with Joseph's dream of the sheaves of grain and the sun, moon, and stars—with all of which he was familiar. The butler dreamed of the grapevine and pressing of grapes into the cup of the king. The baker dreamed of bread trays which he often carried on his head. But all of these scenes of everyday activities were symbols of something greater yet to happen in the lives of the dreamers.

A Zairian pastor came to me during a conference in the interior of Africa and told me his dream. He said that in the dream he was trying to get to God, but there were some little men who were hindering him and he could not succeed in his approach to God. Then a ladder was set up to heaven and with this ladder he was able to get to God. It was evident that this man's desire was to get to know the Lord and his power.

When he told the dream, I did not know what the "little men" represented. I asked the missionary. He thought they might represent pygmies, which was a good rational interpretation. However, it was the Africans who knew what that picture represented. At the head of their village was a little triangular hut about three feet high. In it were placed many sticks. When a man died, a branch would be cut and a stick named after him. These sticks were called "little men" and placed in the hut. The chief told us that when the men of the village went to hunt, they would place an offering at the hut for the success of their venture. What were they doing? They were worshiping the spirit of the dead. Who were the "little men"? The spirits of the dead. What was keeping him from getting to God? It was witchcraft. But in the dream a ladder was set up by which he could get to God. That was exactly what happened at that conference. As we showed the pastors how to obtain the power of Christ, it brought them into the tremendous victory over the powers of evil. The dream, however, had been a riddle to them because they could not understand dreams properly, and it was a riddle to us because we were not familiar with their customs.

Some symbols portrayed general characteristics, such as the ferocious beasts in Daniel's dream, representing powerful nations. Some images were universal, such as the dragon and the serpent representing Satan. Some were beautiful pictures, as of the river with the water of life and luscious fruit hanging from the trees. There seems to be no end to the variety of images that the visions and dreams take to convey their messages. The most common error in the interpretation of a dream is that we take it literally and interpret it rationally. We must avoid that constantly. Rather, we should look at a dream as picture language, perhaps like a cartoon. If you see a political cartoon of an eagle and a bear fighting, you know that it probably speaks symbolically of the United States and Russia at war. So when the dream speaks of animals we inquire immediately to find what that animal represents to the dreamer, and sometimes what it represents in literature, and what its characteristics are.

When we dream of people, ninety-five percent of the time we are not dreaming of them as individuals but of that which they represent. A man dreamed that he was playing tennis with Billy Jean King and was doing terribly. Of course, Billy Jean represented a champion to him. But the champion was a woman. So it seems from the dream that there is a champion within the dreamer and it is the feminine part of him, called the "anima." If he will cooperate with that anima, he can play a good game. That feminine part is also the creative part. This man was doing work which needed creative expression. However, he looked at this problem from the rational point of view ordinarily. As he saw himself in the dream, he saw the conscious part of himself, the ego. The other person—in this case Billy Jean—represented another part of himself. The dream therefore reflected his inner condition and suggested a remedy.

Only rarely is the dream objective, that is, it rarely speaks of the actual individual one dreams about. Dreams about individuals must be handled very carefully. The dream uses natural imagery, and often the most natural interpretation is the correct one. So when one dreams he is falling, he should check to see why he is not on solid ground psychologically. When one dreams that he is not properly dressed, he should think what he is embarrassed or ill at ease about in relation to others. When a woman dreams that she is about to bear a child, it may mean that a new idea or concept is being born within her.

Death in a dream usually does not represent physical death, but the death of a part of one's self. For example, a man dreamed that he was attending a funeral service, but then as he looked he saw that he was in the casket. The dream was picturing the conscious part of him observing the death of another part of himself—which may be good or bad, depending on what part of him had died. On the other hand, when a dream represents physical death, it does so symbolically. To illustrate, a man saw a bird flying in the air and suddenly it hit a wall and it dropped dead. That dream foretold the man's own sudden death, which took place within a very short time. The warnings of a dream are to be taken seriously. However, the dream is not to be interpreted literally—as though the previously mentioned dream was saying that the dreamer's bird would fall dead—but symbolically. And that symbolism must be understood. So the dream speaks simply in picture language, a language which children understand more easily than adults do. To understand a dream, we must become more like little children.

However, we may wonder whether Satan cannot use the dream. Of course, the deceiver will use whatever means he can. However, I have found that we can trust our dreams as we trust our thoughts. We know that Satan can use our thoughts, yet we do not stop thinking. Instead, we yield ourselves to God and trust him to guard our thoughts. The same is true of dreams. However, I have found that wherever people are involved in a great deal of witchcraft, as in the jungles of Africa, South America, and New Guinea where I have been, people may have much trouble with their dreams. Yet it is not the dreams that are wrong, for they still seem to give an accurate reflection of that which is going on inwardly. But Satan's deceit usually comes through a wrong interpretation. Therefore, we need always to place ourselves in God's protection. Then trust him in all things, including your dreams. Do not think that just because there is fear in the dream, therefore Satan is in it. Nebuchadnezzar's dreams were fearful, but they were a true reflection of his inner condition. And they led him to God.

The great reward in dreaming is in getting the right interpretation. The great danger lies in receiving the wrong interpretation. How can we be sure of the right one? God has given us a safe rule for interpreting dreams. We see that rule illustrated in the Bible. If an interpretation is right, the one who has had the dream will know it, though he may not be conscious of it or be able to define it, for the dream is a confirmation of that which we already know. Therefore, never receive an interpretation of your own dream that your heart does not respond to. Never force upon anyone an interpretation of his dream which he cannot agree with inwardly. If we follow that rule we will be quite safe. Pharaoh knew that Joseph's interpretation was right, and as a reward advanced Joseph to a high position. Nebuchadnezzar also knew that Daniel's interpretation was correct, though it had a terrible warning to him, and he honored Daniel for it. Usually we will know immediately if the interpretation is correct, even if we do not understand the dream as a whole. But remember that dreams and visions constitute a language that we must begin to learn, and we do not learn a language in just a few lessons. It takes years to master it.

We see, then, that dreams and visions speak in a universal language to all men—believers and unbelievers alike. They spoke to Pharaoh as well as to Joseph; to Nebuchadnezzar as well as to Daniel. They were a personal language to each one, showing him where his heart stood with respect to the situation in which he was involved. They told him what would happen if he continued in the direction in which he was going. But they spoke in a language foreign to most people today—a language of images and pictures and symbols. But if God speaks in that language to all people, it is our responsibility to learn to understand the language and obey his will. How can we go on learning the higher language of the Spirit if we have not yet learned the elementary language of dreams and visions?

7
How God Speaks
by
His Spirit

When we think about God's speaking through the Scriptures most of us are on familiar ground. When we think of his speaking through dreams and visions some of us may have been a bit frightened. But when we think about God's speaking through his Holy Spirit, we may be familiar with the theory of it and yet find it very hard to explain. We can relate to Jesus as he walked upon earth and taught his disciples, but it is another matter to relate to the Holy Spirit. This is because he is Spirit and not flesh. We are unfamiliar with the spirit world.

A young Indian was our guide deep in the jungle of South America. The missionary told us about the spiritual realm in which he lived. His brother was a witch doctor and his brother-in-law a Christian. He had to make his choice between the two opposing spiritual powers because he had been "chosen" to be the next witch doctor. Through the interpreter he told me. how the spirits approached him in the forest. Often they would come by some audible sign like a knock or a visual movement in the trees, but always it was evident that there was a spiritual force behind it. During that time the Spirit of God also spoke to him about being a Christian. This was an appeal of love which attracted him greatly and won out in the end.

Because he was so constantly approached by the spiritual world, he spoke familiarly of it. He knew both the world of demons, which he feared, and the realm of angels who came to his rescue. His environment very really included the spiritual realm as well as the material, but the spiritual seemed more real.

We must all recognize that we too are dealing with a real world of good and the real world of evil, two realms that Paul clearly distinguished. The one is the realm of the idol or fetish and the demons that gave it power; the other is the realm of Jesus and the Spirit who speaks to us. Some men claimed to speak messages from the Spirit of God, but how could the people really tell if they were from God or from Satan, the great deceiver? Paul said, "Here is the test: no one speaking by the power of the Spirit of God can curse Jesus, and no one can say, 'Jesus is Lord,' and really mean it, unless the Holy Spirit is helping him" (1 Corinthians 12:3).

The spirit behind the evil forces will always curse Jesus, the Son of God, even though temporarily he may even seem to flatter him. (See Acts 16:16-18.) The Holy Spirit of God will always acknowledge that Jesus is Lord. It is the Holy Spirit who wants to reveal God the Father and make Jesus real to us.

The Holy Spirit was there in the process of creation, bringing order out of chaos and light out of darkness. In his relation to man we find a distinct difference between that of the Old Testament and that of the New. In Old Testament days the Spirit came upon men to empower them for great works. When God assigned Moses the task of leading Israel, as more than a million former slaves from Egypt, he gave Moses of his Spirit. We do not know with what voice God spoke to Moses at the burning bush, but we know that Moses recognized the voice. When the burden of leadership became too heavy, Moses complained. He asked that the Lord would kill him rather than requiring him to carry that great load. The Lord replied, "Summon before me seventy of the leaders of Israel; bring them to the Tabernacle, to stand there with you. I will come down and talk with you there and I will take of the Spirit which is on you and will put it upon them also; they will bear the burden of the people along with you, so that you will not have the task alone" (Numbers 11:16, 17). The Lord came down in a cloud and took some of the Spirit that was on Moses and put it on the seventy elders and they prophesied.

When Joshua became jealous of two of the men who prophesied in the camp, we read: "Are you jealous for my sake? I only wish that all of the Lord's people were prophets, and that the Lord would put his Spirit upon them all" (Numbers 11:29). And the Holy Spirit came upon the seventy elders to share the burden of leadership. The gift of prophecy seemed to be a sign that the Holy Spirit had come upon them.

After Israel had settled in the Promised Land, but were still fighting to conquer it, the Spirit of the Lord came upon Othniel and gave him power and wisdom to conquer and rule the people. The Spirit of the Lord also came upon Gideon, enabling him to lead his small army to victory over great hordes of the enemy. Even Samson with his questionable practices still had the Spirit of God come upon him to give him unusual physical strength. We know that the Spirit of God was upon David when he wrote his beautiful songs of prayer and praise. He knew it too, for when he sinned against God he prayed that the Holy Spirit would not be taken from him. (See Psalm 51.)

But it is the prophets who bear the special seal of the Spirit of God upon them. The Spirit of God was upon Elijah and upon Elisha his disciple. In fact Elisha prayed that a double portion of the Spirit that was upon Elijah would come upon him. His prayer was answered. The power in Elisha's life was evident as he multiplied the bread, as he increased the oil, and as he prescribed the cure for Naaman the leper. In fact Elisha was so filled with the Spirit of God that after he died, enough power remained in his buried bones to raise another dead man! (See 2 Kings 13:20, 21.)

Isaiah saw the Lord filling the temple and then received the commission to go to the people who would not listen. Ezekiel saw such fascinating visions from God that he was taken up by them in the glory itself. However it was in the messages of the prophets that there is special evidence of the Spirit of God present with them. Peter said, "This salvation was something the prophets did not fully understand. Though they wrote about it, they had many questions as to what it all could mean" (1 Peter 1:10). The Spirit of God through them gave information concerning the sufferings and glory of Christ that since has been fulfilled. What was given to them by the Spirit was beyond their own comprehension.

The difference between the Holy Spirit's ministry in the Old Testament and his ministry in the New is seen most clearly in the experience of Saul, the first king of Israel. Saul was anointed by Samuel to be king. In the anointing Samuel applied oil as a symbol of the Spirit. Then "as Saul said good-bye and started to go, God gave him a new attitude, and all of Samuel's prophecies came true that day" (1 Samuel 10:9).

When Saul saw the prophets, the Spirit of God came upon him and he began to prophesy too. However, Saul did not prove to be a humble man. He could not stand to see David getting more credit than he. As time went by he became very jealous. One day as Saul was sitting at home listening to David play the harp, suddenly the tormenting spirit from the Lord attacked him. He had his spear in his hand, and hurled it at David in an attempt to kill him. But David dodged the spear and fled, leaving the spear in the wall. Saul then sent troops to David's house to kill him, but again he escaped, and this time he went to the Hill of God with Samuel. Saul sent soldiers to capture David but when they arrived a very strange thing happened. When they saw Samuel and the other prophets prophesying, the Spirit of God came upon them and they began to prophesy. When

Saul learned of that, he sent other soldiers and they too prophesied. This happened a third time. Then Saul, with murder in his heart, went to Rama, demanding, "Where are Samuel and David?" Someone told him they were at Naioth. But on the way to Naioth the Spirit of God came upon Saul and he too began to prophesy! (See 1 Samuel 19:19-23.)

The fact that the Spirit of God had come upon Saul so that he prophesied did not mean that his heart was changed at that time. He still was a murderer at heart and continued to be so.

So the Spirit of God was upon Saul but not within him filling his heart with love. Evidently in those days the Spirit of God came upon a prophet, who would usually cooperate; yet if he did not, the Spirit of God would still use him as an instrument for good. This was true of Balaam, as we have seen. This may also explain the prophecy that Caiaphas made concerning Jesus before the crucifixion. The prophecy proved to be true and yet he with the other leaders concurred in the plan to kill Jesus. "And one of them, Caiaphas, who was High Priest that year, said, 'You stupid idiots— let this one man die for the people—why should the whole nation perish?' " John then explains that "this prophecy that Jesus should die for the entire nation came from Caiaphas in his position as High Priest—he didn't think of it by himself, but was inspired to say it" (John 11:49-51).

In the Old Testament God spoke through his Spirit, sometimes coming upon men in spite of the attitude of their hearts. Then with the coming of Jesus we find something new. Jesus, filled with the Spirit without measure, walked in perfect obedience to the Father. But to do the work that the Father had given him, he received power through the Holy Spirit at his baptism. And when he had performed his mighty miracles he testified that it was by God's Spirit he had done so. Once, in response to the Pharisees' accusations he said, "If I am casting out demons by the Spirit of God, then the Kingdom of God has arrived among you. One cannot rob Satan's kingdom without first binding Satan. Only then can his demons be cast out!" (Matthew 12:28, 29).

Jesus furthermore spoke with an authority that amazed

his hearers. He did not say, as the prophets had, "Thus said the Lord." Instead he said, "I say unto you." The authority was within him by the Spirit of God. Before Jesus left his disciples he promised them that they too would receive the same Holy Spirit if they would love and obey him. "He is the Holy Spirit, the Spirit who leads into all truth. The world at large cannot receive him, for it isn't looking for him and doesn't recognize him. But you do, for he lives with you now and some day shall be in you" (John 15:17).

Jesus also told his disciples that the Spirit would indwell them and give them power to speak for him. Just before he left them he said that all authority in heaven and on earth had been given to him. Then he told them to go with that authority. And yet they were not to go until the Spirit of God who gave them that authority had come. "But when the Holy Spirit has come upon you, you will receive power to testify about me with great effect, to the people in Jerusalem, throughout Judea, in Samaria, and to the ends of the earth, about my death and resurrection" (Acts 1:8).

In obedience to Jesus, the disciples waited until the Holy Spirit filled them at Pentecost. Immediately afterwards the same kind of authority that was in Jesus was in them, for Jesus had said, "In solemn truth I tell you, anyone believing in me shall do the same miracles I have done, and even greater ones, because I am going to be with the Father" (John 14:12).

At Pentecost the disciples spoke out their praises to God in language that was unknown to them but understood by the hearers. Peter explained the happening, and as a result three thousand people repented and believed in Jesus as the Christ. That result was at least numerically greater than any of the recorded results of Jesus' own preaching. The Spirit of God had indeed come to the disciples.

However when Peter spoke he did not say, "Thus saith the Lord," as the Old Testament prophets had done, but he spoke as one who had the authority within him. We read that when Peter was challenged about his authority after the cripple was healed, he stated without apology that "it was done in the name and power of Jesus from Nazareth, the

Messiah, the man you crucified—but God raised back to life again. It is by his authority that this man stands here healed!" (Acts 4:10). The authority they had was in Jesus, and the Spirit of God made Jesus real to them.

As God now spoke by his Spirit through the disciples there was no "Thus saith the Lord" formula, but they spoke in a common manner. They were not having to defend themselves. God was their defense. When they prayed, "Grant to your servants great boldness," it was a boldness to name the name of Jesus, whereupon God produced the evidence of his presence within them. There was no brashness, for there was no self-seeking.

In the same way when the apostle Paul wrote the biblical letters the Spirit of God was with him and spoke through him, even though at the time he was simply writing to a friend. He was aware that God was with him, for he sent blessings and peace from God to them; yet there was no formula to distinguish that from the other writings. The presence of the Spirit of God in the letters became known by the power in them. Even though they were personal letters, they were eventually put alongside the Old Testament Scriptures because of the same evident authority in them. Thus in the New Testament God spoke in common ways through men, and God's power of the Spirit was imbedded within some ordinary-looking writings.

There were also special ways in which God spoke by the Holy Spirit. There were the special manifestations of the Spirit of God, referred to as the gifts of the Spirit.

For to one is given by the Spirit the word of wisdom; to another the word of knowledge by the same Spirit; to another faith by the same Spirit; to another the gifts of healing by the same Spirit; to another the working of miracles; to another prophecy; to another discerning of spirits; to another divers kinds of tongues; but all these worketh that one and the selfsame Spirit; dividing to every man severally as he will (1 Corinthians 12:8-11 KJV).

It was through these gifts that the power of the Holy Spirit was manifest in the life of Jesus and in the church. Jesus had told the disciples, "Go and announce to them that the Kingdom of Heaven is near. Heal the sick, raise the dead, cure the lepers, and cast out demons. Give as freely as you have received" (Matthew 10:7, 8). It was by the power of the Holy Spirit that these supernatural works were to be done. They were to be signs of God's power in the midst of his Church.

Through some of these gifts or abilities the Spirit of God spoke with unusual power. One such was a gift of wisdom. Jesus prepared his disciples for opposition. He also promised them power for the time of need, for he said that they would be arrested, tried, and whipped in the synagogues. That would provide opportunity to give their witness before governors and kings. There a special spiritual provision would be made. "When you are arrested, don't worry about what to say at your trial, for you will be given the right words at the right time. For it won't be you doing the talking—it will be the spirit of your Heavenly Father speaking through you" (Matthew 10:19, 20).

This is seen in the life of Stephen, one of the seven appointed to minister to needy widows in the church. Stephen had been filled with the Spirit and was given grace and power to work miracles and great signs among the people. When he was challenged by those who were evidently better trained than he was, he could not by his natural wisdom answer their arguments. Yet, "none of them were able to stand against Stephen's wisdom and spirit," says Acts 6:10. In this case God spoke using the mind and personality of Stephen but giving words beyond his natural wisdom. The supernatural was absorbed right into the natural so that it looked like the natural but the power was evidently from God.

Silenced by the supernatural wisdom given to Stephen, his opponents did what people sometimes do when they can't answer an argument. They picked up stones and killed him. But Stephen, filled with the Holy Spirit, gazed up into heaven and saw the glory of God and Jesus standing at God's right hand. Thus the word of wisdom given as Jesus had promised was what overcame the arguments of the opposers. One result was that Saul, who was standing by and agreeing with the murder of Stephen, turned about face shortly afterwards and became the great apostle of Stephen's Christ.

Another of the gifts by which the Spirit spoke is the word of knowledge. This became evident as Peter was leading a meeting in which many of the believers were sharing in great joy and with sacrifice. Barnabas had sold his piece of land and brought the money and presented it to the apostles. But there was a man named Ananias, and his wife Sapphira, who sold their property and pretended to bring the money as an offering. Secretly they had kept back part of the money. Peter, discerning this, said, "Ananias, Satan has filled your heart. When you claimed this was the full price, you were lying to the Holy Spirit" (Acts 5:3). The question was not whether they sold the property or whether they gave the money away. The question was about their honesty. They tried to hide their deceit but God found them out. When Ananias heard the Spirit-inspired words of Peter he fell dead and the church was aware that the power of God was upon the disciples. How did Peter know that Ananias and Sapphira were not telling the truth? Evidently the Holy Spirit gave Peter a word of knowledge or insight for the occasion. That word had power so that when he spoke it and Ananias did not repent, God suddenly brought judgment upon him.

The word of knowledge was evident in various ways in the ministry of Jesus. When Jesus, tired and thirsty, sat by Jacob's well, a Samaritan woman came to draw water. She was surprised that he conversed with her. But Jesus soon changed the conversation from the natural to the living water in which she expressed an interest. So he told her to go call her husband and come back. When she replied that she had no husband, Jesus through some special knowledge or insight was able to say to her, "All too true! For you have had five husbands and you aren't even married to the man you're living with now" (John 4:18). The secrets of her life had been revealed, and when she went back to the village and invited the people to come, she said, "Come and meet a man who told me everything I ever did! Can this be the Messiah?" (John 4:29). The whole village turned to Christ after a word showed this woman that the man who spoke to her must be a prophet. The word of knowledge searched out her heart and was a means of bringing her to Christ. And through the same gifts the Spirit would give others supernatural power for witnessing to Jesus.

God spoke by his Spirit through the gift of prophecy in the New Testament as well as the Old. After Pentecost, when Peter spoke to the great crowd that had gathered, he said, " 'In the last days,' God said, 'I will pour out my Holy Spirit upon all mankind, and your sons and daughters shall prophesy and your young men shall see visions, and your old men dream dreams. Yes, the Holy Spirit shall come upon all my servants, men and women alike, and they shall prophecy' " (Acts 2:17, 18). In the book of Acts we see that the Spirit through prophecy predicted a famine, confirmed a call, warned an apostle, revealed a spiritual gift, and gave a revelation of the future. And after a new church had been established,

> *Some prophets came down from Jerusalem to Antioch, and one of them, named Agabus, stood up in one of the meetings to predict by the Spirit that a great famine was coming upon the land of Israel. (This was fulfilled during the reign of Claudius.) So the believers decided to send relief to the Christians in Judea, each giving as much as he could. This they did, consigning their gifts to Barnabas and Paul to take to the elders of the church in Jerusalem (Acts 11:27-30).*

In this instance the prophet visiting the church was suddenly directed by the Spirit of God to give a word concerning the famine he was warned about. The church received that word and acted upon it, so that by the time the famine came the food had already arrived. In such a practical way God spoke through prophecy to the church.

Later the time came to send out the first missionaries from the church. They would need to have a call from the Lord which was both personal and also recognized by the church. The new church at Antioch now had its first prophets. Luke reports: "One day as these men were worshiping and fasting the Holy Spirit said, 'Dedicate Barnabas and Paul for a special job I have for them' " (Acts 13:2). God called Paul and Barnabas privately but they waited for confirmation to come, and must have been encouraged by the word of prophecy. In the same way the prophecy of the church was confirmed by Paul and Barnabas. "So after more fasting and prayer, the men laid their hands on them—and sent them on their way" (Acts 13:3).

God spoke through prophecy also to warn the apostles of impending danger. We will remember how Agabus the prophet warned Paul about going to Jerusalem (Acts 21). And just as it was told, so it happened. He was bound and imprisoned when he went there. But through the prophecy he had been warned.

The laying on of hands was not a mere ritual in the early church. When they laid hands on men and prayed for them they expected God to speak through them and give a message to the one for whom they were praying. Luke tells us that in their travels they came to Lystra and found Timothy, a believing young man who was well spoken of. He was one whom Paul wanted as a traveling companion—one whom he could train to follow up his work. Later he called the elders of the church together and they laid hands on Timothy and God gave a word of prophecy concerning him. The prophecy said that he was to receive a spiritual gift. This gift was to be exercised in ministry. Evidently Timothy was not doing that, so Paul wrote Timothy a letter in which he said, "Be sure to use the abilities God has given you through his prophets when the elders of the church laid their hands upon your head" (1 Timothy 4:14). It was the prophecy with the laying on of hands that awakened them to the gift that was given to Timothy. But Paul knew that it had to be exercised in order to come to fruition. How aware the church must have been of God's presence as he spoke through his prophets giving direction, encouragement, or promise according to their needs!

The gift of prophecy is defined by the apostle Paul as primarily a ministry to build up the body of Christ. Paul says, "One who prophesies, preaching the messages of God, is helping others grow in the Lord, encouraging and comforting them" (1 Corinthians 14:3). Therefore God spoke by his Spirit through prophecy in the teaching and encouraging and comforting of his people. So in that sense the letters of Paul and Peter and John and Jude were part of the great prophecy of God by his Spirit. It seems that the difference between teaching with all the natural powers of the mind alone and teaching in the power of the Holy Spirit directing the mind, is that the latter only is prophecy. Prophecy has the element of the supernatural in it, even when the material taught is in the natural realm.

The Spirit of God lifts teaching to a higher level, thus bringing even geography, mathematics, and the sciences into a freedom not limited to the wisdom of man. Even the teaching of Scripture can become uninteresting and powerless when it is without the power of the Spirit of God. But when Jesus taught the Scriptures he did so by the power of the Holy Spirit lifting it right out of the bondage of legalism and giving it a power to set men free. Therefore Paul encouraged the Roman Christians to do this kind of teaching. "God has given each of us the ability to do certain things well," he wrote. "So if God has given you the ability to prophesy, then prophesy whenever you can—as often as your faith is strong enough to receive a message from God" (Romans 12:6).

That was the big difference between the teaching of Jesus and that of the scribes and Pharisees. "The crowds were amazed at Jesus' sermons, for he taught as one who had great authority, and not as their Jewish leaders" (Matthew 7:28, 29). This was also evident in Jesus' followers. When the Jewish council recognized that these uneducated non-professionals had been with Jesus, "they were amazed and realized what being with Jesus had done for them" (Acts 4:13).

Prophecy is not bound to time. Through it God often predicts the future. By the word of prophecy Paul and Peter and John and Jude all spoke of the future and of the need to prepare for things to come. In his second letter Peter says: "No prophecy recorded in Scripture was ever thought up by the prophet himself. It was the Holy Spirit within these godly men who gave them true messages from God." Therefore he calls upon them to pay close attention to that which they have written. "So we have seen and proved that what the prophets said came true" (2 Peter 1:19-21).

Of course, Peter went on to say that in his people's history there were false prophets as well as the true prophets of the Lord. He said too that there will be false teachers. Tests of prophecy are always needed. These we will consider carefully in a later chapter. But we see that God spoke in a miraculous way through the gift of prophecy.

Then another special way that God spoke by his Spirit was through revelation. God gave Paul the message of the gospel to the Gentiles by this means. "I must make it clear to you, my friends," he said, "that the gospel you heard me preach is no human invention. I did not take it over from any man; no man taught it me; I received it through a revelation of Jesus Christ" (Galatians 1:11, 12 NEB). Paul was so sure of the message given to him by this revelation that only afterwards did he go to Peter and the other apostles, who confirmed it.

The apostle John had a similar experience which he mentioned in his book containing his letters to the seven churches of Asia Minor. "This book unveils Christ," he said. God revealed these things to his servant John in a vision. Then an angel sent from heaven explained the vision's meaning. John wrote it all down—the words of God and Jesus Christ and everything he heard and saw.

Of this revelation John wrote: "If you read this prophecy aloud to the church, you will receive a special blessing from the Lord. Those who listen to it being read and do what it says will also be blessed. For the time is near when these things will all come true" (Revelation 1:1-3). There he too was lifted up into heaven and beyond the dimensions of time, where he saw things that will yet come to pass. In the last chapter of his book he said, "Then the angel said to me, 'These words are trustworthy and true: "I am coming soon!" God, who tells his prophets what the future holds, has sent his angel to tell you this will happen soon. Blessed are those who believe it and all else written in the scroll' " (Revelation 22:6, 7). And one of the last verses of his book says, "The Spirit and the bride say, 'Come.' Let each one who hears them say the same, 'Come.' Let the thirsty one come—anyone who wants to; let him come and drink the Water of Life without charge" (Revelation 22:6, 7, 17).

Thus was fulfilled Jesus' promise: "I am telling you these things now while I am still with you. But when the Father sends the Comforter instead of me—and by the Comforter I mean the Holy Spirit—he will teach you much, as well as remind you of everything I myself have told you" (John 14:25, 26). Also fulfilled was this other promise of Jesus: "When the Holy Spirit, who is truth, comes, he shall guide you into all truth, for he will not be presenting his own ideas, but will be passing on to you what he has heard. He will tell you about the future" (John 16:13).

It is no wonder that Jesus told them not to leave Jerusalem but to wait there for that which the Father promised. "But when the Holy Spirit has come upon you, you will receive power to testify about me with great effect, to the people in Jerusalem, throughout Judea, in Samaria, and to the ends of the earth, about my death and resurrection" (Acts 1:8).

THREE

DISCERNING THE VOICE OF GOD

8
The Voices
We Hear

In our rationalistic society, permeated by Aristotelian philosophy and Freudian psychology, we are not supposed to hear voices. This attitude comes from the knowledge that when a person is psychologically unbalanced he may hear voices that tell him lies about himself and cause him to do destructive things. Such voices, of course, are not to be obeyed. Yet, in another sense all of us hear voices. Aware of the inner conflict that exists within us, we hear the voice of our own desires, the voice of conscience, the voice of public opinion, the voice of authority, the voice of temptation, and many other voices. Such voices, of course, are not usually audible. They may come as thoughts, impressions, compulsions, or hunches. Among these also is the voice of God. This we must learn to distinguish from all the others.

Let us look to see where these voices come from. First, there is the voice of the five senses. What these senses take in

we call facts. Knowledge from that realm we say is undeni-
able because we have a physical body and live in a physical
world. We can see things with our eyes, hear them with our
ears, feel them, smell them, taste them. We live in the world
around us by the messages that come from these senses.

Second, there are voices of the mind. These come from
our own reasoning, or the logic of others, plus all that comes
from material science, philosophy, and psychology. This
overwhelmingly vast area of knowledge comes mostly
through the mind. It is a strong voice loudly heard throughout the western world, the voice of reason.

Third, there is the voice of the emotions—the exclama-
tion or groan of despair. That voice comes not from our
reason but from our emotions. Often our feelings have little
to do with the thoughts of our minds. This voice evaluates
things from a personal angle, whether good or bad.

Fourth, there is a mysterious voice of intuition. Intuition
tells us what we know will happen—things we do not know
through our five senses nor through the reasonings of the
mind nor from our feelings. We just know it. Our reason
may often silence the voice of intuition, our observations
may deny it, our feelings may ignore it so that we do not
obey that voice; but even when we disobey it and fail in the
process, we often know what we should have done. All these
voices from the five senses, from reason, from the feelings,
and from intuition are valid. Each of us has learned to obey
or to ignore these voices in the process of seeking our guidance. They have all been with us from the beginning.

Then there are the voices that speak from our training
and the various influences which have affected our lives.
There is the voice of conscience, which speaks of that which
we received in our upbringing. Conscience tells us what is
right and wrong, but it is not necessarily as accurate as the
truth of God. Conscience merely tells us what is right and
wrong according to *the way we have been taught.* Yet conscience
can be a very strong voice keeping us in a narrow way, at least
the narrow way of our traditions.

There is also the voice of authority, such as the voice of a
father or mother or a teacher. Even after that authority fig-

ure has died, his or her voice may still "speak" loudly whenever we are about to make certain kinds of choices. These and many more voices we hear within us day after day. Any of these may be positive voices which God can use as his voice to us. On the other hand any of these voices can be misdirected and become the voice of the enemy for our destruction.

At times God may show us things through our five senses, as he did when some of the men of Israel saw that the land of Canaan was good, and they knew that God wanted them to take it. We too may see certain material things and feel assured that God has told us to take them. God may also speak to us through our power of reasoning. For example, he warned Israel by reminding them of what happened to them when they ignored the laws of God. That is, he reasoned with them that they must obey his laws. He expects us to use our minds and think through our problems.

God may also speak through our emotions and feelings, even as Jesus had compassion on the multitude who were hungry and were as sheep without a shepherd. His compassion demanded that he must do something for them. And then God may speak through our intuition. The more we yield to God the more he is able to correct our natural intuition and give us true spiritual perception. As God said through Isaiah, "If you leave God's paths and go astray, you will hear a Voice behind you say, 'No, this is the way; walk here' " (Isaiah 30:21).

But we are aware that we must also deal with the tempter, who can make the senses receive something that the voices are not saying. He may blind us so that we cannot even see the natural consequences of our disobedience. This happened to the small remnant of Israel who were spared from the captivity but were afraid to trust God for their security. The women present, and the men whose wives had burned incense to idols, said that they would not listen to Jeremiah's messages from God for them. Instead they said, "We will burn incense to the 'Queen of Heaven' and sacrifice to her just as much as we like—just as we and our fathers before us, and our kings and princes have always done in the cities of

Judah and in the streets of Jerusalem; for in those days we had plenty to eat and we were well off and happy!"

They could not see that they had caused their own troubles but said, "Ever since we quit burning incense to the 'Queen of Heaven' and stopped worshiping her we have been in great trouble and have been destroyed by sword and famine." But Jeremiah said, "The very reason all these terrible things have befallen you is because you have burned incense and sinned against the Lord and refused to obey him" (Jeremiah 44:15-23). They were as blinded as a man who cannot see the connection between his alcohol consumption and his family's suffering, or between his gambling and his own financial difficulties.

Then, too, the enemy may use reason to deceive us as he did in the Garden, saying to Adam and Eve, "Has God really said that you shall not eat of every tree in the garden?" By raising that question he led them into sin. How many have been trapped by the enemy through the philosophies of this world, so that their reasonings become evil and rebellious toward God! Our emotions, too, can become captives of the enemy. While God wants to fill our lives with joy and happiness, the enemy tempts us to make "the pursuit of happiness" our consuming goal. Satan offers us immediate but temporary happiness. God's joys often must wait, but they are permanent.

Intuition, that faculty that enables us to listen to the voice of our inner beings, may also entice us to listen to the enemy. The "voice" of the psychopath may be the voice of pride saying, "I am God" or it may be the voice of fear saying, "They are after me." The wrongly trained conscience can easily become the voice of prejudice or even hatred, so that a man hates the Catholic or the Protestant or the Jew or the Arab or the black or the white or the white collar or the blue collar person. And the voice of authority can become the voice of a Stalin or a Hitler, if the authority is misused.

How can we discern the voice of God from all of these voices? How do we hear God? Is the voice audible? Do we hear it with our physical ears? No, for God is Spirit and it is by his Spirit that he communicates with our spirits. Our spirits "hear" him. God's message may come through the mind, the emotions, the intuition, or even the five senses. But it is the spirit in us that hears and recognizes the voice to be the voice of God. Therefore, the question whether it is "audible" is irrelevant to the hearer. I sometimes ask one who insists that he heard an audible voice, whether others nearby heard it. If so, it was audible—as with Paul's experience when he met the Lord. In that case "they heard the sound of someone's voice but saw no one" (Acts 9:7). Sometimes it may be the reverse as the presence is seen but the voice is not heard. But it does seem that an audible voice is comparatively rare. The important question is not "Was it audible?" but "Was it the voice of God?"

We do not know our spirits. Our bodies, with their five senses, we are acquainted with. Our souls, with their intellect, emotions, and will, we understand. But the world has not taught us about our spirits. Paul, who was taught by the Spirit of God, says that just as no one can know the deepest thoughts of a person but he himself, so no one can know the deep thoughts of God but God's own Spirit. It is this Spirit that he gives us to enable us to know the deep secrets of God. The natural man cannot understand this because he has only a human spirit, but the believer has received the Spirit of God. "Strange as it seems, we Christians actually do have with us a portion of the very thoughts and mind of Christ" (1 Corinthians 2:10-16).

A person's spirit is awakened to God when by a spiritual birth he is born into the Kingdom of God. It is then that he comes into communication with God. "For his Holy Spirit speaks to us deep in our hearts, and tells us that we really are God's children" (Romans 8:16). That is where real communication with God begins.

When we look at the members of the Godhead and the parts of manhood, we can see how our communication with God comes about. We know that man cannot reach God through his physical body. He cannot climb up into heaven and see God. In answer to the cosmonaut who said that there was no God, because he was in outer space and he saw no God there, someone suggested, more tragically than humorously, that if he had stepped out of his capsule he would have met God very quickly. We know that such reasoning as the cosmonaut made is ridiculous, for it is not with our physical senses that we become aware of him.

Most of religion is man's attempt to reach God through the soul. Within the soul the mind, the emotions, and the will are at work. Some think that man can discover God with his mind and so they write a great deal of theology. But a knowledge of all the theology in the world only tells us *about* God and cannot of itself bring us into a living relationship *with* God. Others say we may reach him if only we will allow our emotions to be expressed sufficiently. But no matter how ecstatic we become, our emotions alone do not bring us into contact with God. Elijah proved this to the prophets of Baal. (See 1 Kings 18.) Still others think it is a matter of the will, and think that they can *determine* to get through to God. But our wills alone cannot bring us into fellowship with God.

God the Father is immortal, invisible, and beyond human comprehension. But the Father has revealed himself through his Son. The Son speaks to us by the Holy Spirit. When the Spirit of God awakens our spirit we are born of God. It is then that the Spirit of God speaks to our spirits and assures us that we are children of God. It is then that he illumines our minds and corrects our thinking. Then he directs our emotions to him, and our wills are then yielded to his will, and even our physical bodies can feel the effect of the Spirit of God revealing the Father and the Son to our whole beings.

When we know that the voice of God is perceived by our spirits, we have a basis for distinguishing that voice from all others. As we come to recognize that voice, we will not be concerned whether it is audible or inaudible, whether it is revealed by voice or by dream, or through the reproof of a friend or through the Scriptures; we just know it is the voice of God.

But again it may be asked, how will we know whether we have heard the voice of God. The answer is: we will know that just as we know our other spiritual realities. Those who have experienced forgiveness know when the guilt of their sins was taken away. Those who have new life in Christ know that they are born again. But what about the person who says there is no such reality because he has not experienced it? A blind man cannot know what the color red is, but his noncomprehension does not make the color nonexistent. So also the natural man's inability to understand the spiritual realm does not make it nonexistent, though to him it may indeed be incomprehensible.

The apostle Paul said, "But you are not like that. You are controlled by your new nature if you have the Spirit of God living in you. (And remember that if anyone doesn't have the Spirit of Christ living in him, he is not a Christian at all)" (Romans 8:9). I am speaking to those who have experienced the new life in Christ. "For all who are led by the Spirit of God are sons of God....For his Holy Spirit speaks to us deep in our hearts, and tells us that we really are God's children" (Romans 8:14, 16). So by the Spirit of God within us, we recognize the voice of the Spirit of God speaking to us.

Are there dangers in this spiritual realm since we know so little about it? Most assuredly there are, but there are also precautions that can make it safe. All the dangers of flying have not kept our planes on the ground. We choose rather to take the precautions and minimize the risk, though risk there always will be. So it is in the spiritual realm. A good friend, acquainted with both the spiritual realm and the field of psychology, says, "The spiritual realm is a dangerous realm, but it is more dangerous to stay out of it." In another chapter we'll look at the safeguards for spiritual guidance.

Let us now look at the reason why we must carefully learn to discern the voice of God. We know that Satan will outrightly oppose us or tempt us into sin. Satan's opposition and his temptations are not too difficult to recognize, for we can usually check that out by the Scriptures, or by the gift of discernment. But when we ourselves get in the way of our hearing, it is harder for us to discern. I remember the time I was invited by a friend to join a little business venture. The "word" that I got from the Lord encouraged me. But I soon learned that that word was from my own desires and not from the Lord at all. Our desires can greatly influence what we seem to hear.

Let us see how the voice of God comes to us. We may think we hear it directly without any interference. But let us imagine that God has a message for us in a sermon. See how it is filtered through our personality. We hear it with our ears, then our mind wrestles with it, shaving it off here and there to fit into our rational concepts. Then our emotions are aroused and the message becomes highly colored by the memory of a past unfortunate experience. Then the will has to decide whether to accept the limited message.

Take an example from the Old Testament. In the days of the Judges, when man had gone far astray, God wanted a man whom he could use. Hannah almost picked up that desire of God, but her response was distorted by her own desires for a child. She prayed that God would give her a child. No answer came. She pled with God. Nothing happened. Finally she became so desperate that she let go of her own will and desires, caught sight of God's desire, and asked God for a son whom she would give to him. Immediately God said yes. God gave her that son, Samuel, who became the great prophet.

At first Hannah had not heard all that God was saying because she was too occupied with her own desires. When she got beyond her own desires, she was able to pick up the voice of God more clearly. For Hannah and for us too, the voice of God is something like the rain. The rain falls from heaven in all purity, but then it becomes defiled in the atmosphere and mingled with earth's soil. Before it can be received back into the heavens it must be purified. So the word from God is pure as it comes from his mouth, but it becomes defiled with our desires, prejudice, and unbelief. Before it can be received again in heaven and answered, it must be purified.

It is evident that our personality traits enter into our hearing as well as into our speaking. When someone gives a word of prophecy that is full of *thee's* and *thou's* and *thus saith the Lord's,* then we can guess that he is influenced by the language of the King James Version of the Bible. When another in a word of prophecy uses ordinary everyday language we know that he communes with God *that* way. In the Bible we see that the language of John and Peter, the fishermen, was different from the language of Paul, the highly educated former Pharisee and member of the Sanhedrin. God uses our individual differences and communicates through us in spite of our personality quirks.

But prejudice may distort our hearing, for the word *hearing* implies more than simply receiving the message. In the German language, the word *hören* implies receiving the message and obeying it. We remember that Jesus had told the disciples that they were to go out to the Gentiles, but they had not gone. When Peter had the vision of the sheet that was let down to him with the animals that the Jews would not eat, he learned that it was his prejudice that had kept him from "hearing" what God was saying to him. In like manner it has been difficult for us as Protestants and Catholics to hear what God is saying through the other. Often we have already made up our minds what the other person believes, without hearing him personally. Thus our personal prejudices stand in the way of the communication that God could use to bring about the unity in his body by his Spirit.

We may find our personality traits influence what we hear from God in another even more general way. For example, the logical, rational thinking person who analyzes and organizes his work expects to hear God in that way. An extremely rational Christian may direct his missionary gift to a mission that can produce "the most results per dollar." He measures the work of God by the world's measuring stick of bigness and success. While being very sincere and deeply committed, he hears only that which is consistent with his reasoning. He may well have caught a part of God's desire, yet narrowed it greatly by his own mode of thinking.

A data-oriented person can see a need and count the money and know just how far that that money will take him. He cannot believe that God is telling him to go beyond the money he can see. He can very easily imagine all the possibilities of catastrophe if he does so. Church treasurers are usually chosen on the basis of that ability. We need to keep good accounts. But we must also be able to see by faith that which God sees and says, and we need to act on what he says whether or not it fits our mode of thinking.

We all appreciate the one who has developed a strong sensitivity to the feelings of other people, one who likes harmony, who can persuade, conciliate, and help other persons appreciate themselves. However, the one who is so strongly sensitive to the feelings of others may also be unduly influenced by their thinking. Therefore, he may hear only what will please others. A person with an exaggerated sensitivity to feelings will have a hard time hearing God tell him to do something that others fear or disapprove.

Then there is the intuitive person. He may be the one who is first to hear God speak. He may be receiving visions that give direction to the church. He may receive a word of prophecy more quickly than others. I have a friend who is a sincere and dedicated young man but who in his early experience was directed mainly by intuition. When he invited Christ into his life he naturally opened to Christ that part of his personality particularly. And he was eager to hear from the Lord and to follow him. One day as he was driving his car, he heard a voice say to him, "If you really trust God you can close your eyes when you drive." He listened to that voice and obeyed it. As a result, he had an accident, as you'd expect.

When the police questioned him, he told them why he had the accident. The police then took his driver's license from him and the judge turned him over to a psychiatrist. He could not get his driver's license back until the psychiatrist approved. The psychiatrist, however, said that anyone who heard voices was schizophrenic.

Do you see the two extremes to which one's view of this subject might go? If what the psychiatrist said was true, if *anyone* who hears voices is schizophrenic, then all of the men of the Bible who had communion with God were psychiatric cases, for they heard God speak. But if what that young man heard was valid, then we know that voices cannot be depended upon. How can we know whether to trust a voice we hear?

Consider the voice that told the young man he could close his eyes when he drove. If that was not the voice of God, was it the voice of Satan? Very likely. We know that the enemy takes advantage of every situation that he can. But what gave Satan that advantage? Was it not the fact that the man was not listening with his whole person? If he had simply checked the voice of intuition with his five senses and looked at the road and the traffic, he could have known that he could not drive with his eyes closed. Had he used his reason, it could have told him not to do that. If he had asked others how they felt about it, and been sensitive to their suggestions, he would undoubtedly have avoided the accident. But he did not let his whole self into the act of decision making, so the enemy took advantage.

Jesus said, "The Lord our God is the one and only God. And you must love him with all your heart and soul and mind and strength" (Mark 12:30). All of our faculties are to be involved in listening to God, hearing him and obeying him.

I was able to direct the young man to another psychiatrist—one who believes it is perfectly normal to hear voices, that is, that we all hear conflicting voices at times. The second psychiatrist was able to recommend that the young man receive the license again. That young man has learned and is growing. God did not reject him for his lack of understanding. Neither does God reject the shortsighted treasurer. Paul's words apply to both:

> *In the same way, we can see and understand only a little about God now, as if we were peering at his reflection in a poor mirror; but someday we are going to see him in his completeness, face to face. Now all that I know is hazy and blurred, but then I will see everything clearly, just as clearly as God sees into my heart right now (1 Corinthians 13:12).*

We may marvel that God would use any of us, so imperfectly do we hear and obey him. However, God chooses to work with vessels of clay. It is important that we do not presume to be what we are not. God has given us his Spirit, who himself is perfect, and we can have real communication with God; but the communication is still far from perfect because communication depends partly on the recipient, and we recipients are imperfect. Anyone who says that he hears God perfectly is saying that there is no interference within him to receive the voice of God—his whole person is in full balance, there is no bias or prejudice, no selfish desire or ambition, his will is in complete alignment with the will of God. I know of only One who could say that, and we must measure ourselves by him. Therefore, we must continue to walk humbly before him. We must seek to hear him as he speaks to us, but we must be willing to receive correction when we make mistakes in reception, knowing that he treats us with love as his children.

9
The Voice
of God
and Its
Many Inflections

"Our future will begin with a call from space." This was the closing sentence of a recent documentary about research on interplanetary communication. Though many do not recognize it, that voice from outer space has already spoken, and it can be heard by man. It is the voice of God.

Though all humans can hear that voice, the recognizableness of that voice has been lost in the babble of man's commerce and philosophy. Occasionally that voice breaks through the din in a time of tragedy. Then we know that God has spoken. But such a breakthrough generally comes after a great loss has already taken place.

Men and women need to hear God's voice more than occasionally. We need to enter into frequent communication with the One who is speaking. Such communication is the interchange of life, and a sign of hope. I learned this at the hospital. As a hospital chaplain, I found it necessary to get an estimate of the patient's spiritual condition so that I could help him further. In order to do that I needed to ask the right question. If I asked whether he belonged to a church, his answer might indicate that he had taken a spiritual step. On the other hand, it might only indicate a gesture made to the church community or to his parents, not necessarily to God. If I asked whether he had been baptized, his answer might suggest an act of faith on the part of his parents or himself, but it might not indicate whether he had responded to it. If I asked whether he was "saved" or "born again," the question itself would have a different meaning to some than to others. I found a question, however, that gave me a clue to the spiritual condition of the patient's life within. I asked him whether his communication with God was one-way communication or two-way. If it is one-way, he talks with God only. If it is two-way communication, he talks with God and also hears from him. When I found someone who experienced two-way communication with God, I had an idea that there was real life within him.

It is by his voice that God communicates with man. The very word "voice" is from the root meaning to call out with a sound. That is the word used so many times of both God and man. We know what the voice of man is like. What is the voice of God like?

It may seem strange to us that a man could be looking at a burning bush, surprised that it is not consumed, and hear a voice out of it that tells him that this is holy ground and that the voice is the voice of God speaking to him. Anyone reporting such an experience today would be in danger of being hustled off to a mental hospital. Yet, as surprised as Moses must have been, he knew he was hearing the voice of God. In fact, he covered his face with his hands, for he was afraid to look at God.

From the bush the voice said, "Now I am going to send you to Pharaoh to demand that he let you lead my people out of Egypt." Moses did not ignore that word, nor did he think that he was losing his mind. Instead he answered that voice by arguing that he was not the person for such a task. Though God said that he would be with him, Moses asked,

"If I go to the people of Israel and tell them that their fathers' God has sent me, they will ask, 'Which God are you talking about?' What shall I tell them?" (Exodus 3:13). The conversation then goes on until Moses reluctantly accepts his assignment. If that had not been the voice of God, what a fool Moses would have become before Pharaoh. But in spite of Moses' many questions, he knew immediately that this was the voice of God, and he obeyed the instructions.

Soon after God created Adam and Eve, he and they were in conversation together. Even after they sinned and were embarrassed, they heard the voice of the Lord God as he was walking in the garden. The invisible, eternal God was just as real to them as though they could physically see him and hear him. "The Lord called to Adam, 'Why are you hiding?' And Adam replied, 'I heard you coming and didn't want you to see me naked. So I hid.' 'Who told you you were naked?' the Lord God asked. 'Have you eaten fruit from the tree I warned you about?'" Even though the conversation becomes threatening to Adam, he continues. "'Yes,' Adam admitted, 'but it was the woman you gave me who brought me some, and I ate it.' Then the Lord God asked the woman, 'How could you do such a thing?'" (Genesis 3:9-13). So God and man were in conversation from the beginning. God even talked with the serpent.

The voice of God sounded different at different times. Sometimes it was like a whisper but sometimes it was a thunderous roar. Let us see what it sounded like to the men of the Bible. When God prepared Israel to receive the Law there was a terrible storm with thunder, lightning, a descending cloud, and a blast like a ram's horn. The people trembled before God when he descended in a fire and the mountain burned like a furnace and shook. Then "as the trumpet blast grew louder and louder, Moses spoke and God thundered his reply" (Exodus 16:19).

Concerning that most unusual experience, Moses said later, "In all history, going back to the time when God created man upon the earth, search from one end of the heavens to the other to see if you can find anything like this: An entire nation heard the voice of God speaking to it from fire, as you did, and lived!" (Deuteronomy 4:32, 33). In this instance God's voice must have been something like the trumpet blast or the roar of the breakers that the apostle John heard centuries later, when he was an exile on the island of Patmos.

When Jesus was nearing his death he was greatly troubled, wanting to be delivered from the coming suffering but knowing that he had come for that purpose. Then he talked to God his Father in prayer, " 'Father, bring glory and honor to your name.' Then a voice spoke from heaven saying, 'I have already done this, and I will do it again' " (John 12:28). In this instance, though the voice was audible, it sounded to some like thunder and to others like the voice of an angel.

Think also of the day when the risen and ascended Christ confronted Paul, the persecuter of the Christians, who was to become the great apostle to the Gentiles. Luke tells us that when Paul was nearing Damascus a bright light shone upon him and he fell to the ground when he heard a voice speaking to him: " 'Paul! Paul! Why are you persecuting me?' 'Who is speaking, sir?' Paul asked. And the voice replied, 'I am Jesus, the one you are persecuting! Now get up and go into the city and await my further instructions' " (Acts 9:4-6).

In this amazing experience all the men heard the sound of the voice, but only Paul understood it and only he saw the vision. In Scripture we do not find many accounts of the voice of God coming in such an audible way to man. In fact, we may be quite surprised at the diversity of the ways in which people did hear God.

The voice of the Lord sounded to David as a tornado or hurricane that felled the great cedars of Lebanon. "So powerful is his voice; so full of majesty. It breaks down the cedars. It splits the giant trees of Lebanon. It shakes Mount Lebanon and Mount Sirion. They leap and skip before him like young calves!" (Psalm 29:4-6).

Such was the mighty wind that blew in Zaire. We had been invited to teach African pastors by groups of fifty in the interior of that country for two months. Through the prayer of the missionaries and the prophecy of the Lord to them, the Lord had promised revival before we arrived. From the beginning of our ministry it became evident that God's Spirit was moving among us. The African pastors had really turned to Christ with all their hearts. They had rejected the power of witchcraft and all its deception and hatred. They had been freed from witchcraft's power but had not yet known of the greater power of God. When we introduced the gifts and ministry of the Holy Spirit they were eager to receive that kind of power which worked through love. In the evening as we heard them singing, in their native dialect, *"Fulleza, Fulleza!"* ("Fill me now! Fill me now!"), we knew that God had created in them a great thirst for the rivers of living water which Jesus had promised to pour out on those who believe.

Conviction of sin and deep repentance came early. The work of God in their lives was deep. They confessed their sins to one another, children confessing to their teachers, adults confessing to their pastors. Women told how they had stolen from their neighbors' gardens. Men repented of immoral acts. They began to pay debts, to the utter astonishment of the unbelievers. As the wind of the Spirit swept across the borders of their land, a neighboring priest found so many people paying bad debts that he asked the leaders to come to his area. As these pastors were filled with the Holy Spirit, they received power of which they had not even known. The revival continued long after we had left. A missionary pilot wrote to tell about one of these pastors, not as great a preacher as some of the African pastors are, who was filled with the Spirit. As that pastor preached in his area, the Holy Spirit produced such great conviction of sin that hundreds of repentant people rejected fetishes in which they had long trusted. The native pastor then asked the missionary pilot to fly in two neighboring pastors to help him with baptism. Examining the baptismal candidates thoroughly to check the reality of their faith, the pastors eliminated five hundred who they felt were not properly prepared. Then in one day they baptized 762 from one pastor's field. That was the result of the voice of the Lord through an African pastor—a voice that broke "the cedars of Lebanon and shook Mount Lebanon and Mount Sirion."

The Old Testament prophet Amos heard the voice of the Lord in a frightening manner. It was like the roar of a lion. Amos was a stranger to the court of the king. He was a herdsman whom the Lord called to be a prophet. But Amaziah, the priest of Bethel, challenged him. Then Amaziah sent orders to Amos: "Get out of here, you prophet, you! Flee to the land of Judah and do your prophesying there!" (Amos 7:12). But earlier Amos had said, "The Lion has roared—tremble in fear. The Lord God has sounded your doom—I dare not refuse to proclaim it!" (Amos 3:8). And before that, God had said through Amos to Israel: "Would I be roaring as a lion unless I had a reason? The fact is, I am getting ready to destroy you. . . . The alarm has sounded—listen and fear! For I, the Lord, am sending disaster into your land" (Amos 3:4-6).

Perhaps Amos had heard the roar of an attacking lion while he was a herdsman of cattle. It was a roar before which men trembled. Now he had heard the voice of an angry God and he had to prophesy.

Jeremiah heard God in quite a different manner. God had called him to be a spokesman to the nations. It was a great and trying task. Jeremiah was discouraged. Listen to their conversation when God first called him. "The Lord said to me, 'I knew you before you were formed within your mother's womb; before you were born I sanctified you and appointed you as my spokesman to the world.' 'O Lord God!' I said, 'I can't do that! I'm far too young! I'm only a youth!' " But the Lord refused to accept his excuse. " 'Don't say that,' he replied, 'for you will go wherever I tell you to. And don't be afraid of the people, for I, the Lord, will be with you and see you through.' Then he touched my mouth and said, 'See, I have put my words in your mouth!" Then God gave him the assignment to warn the nations and the assurance that by the words of God through him nations would rise and fall. (See Jeremiah 1:4-10.) What authority the voice of God in man can carry!

Jeremiah was moved deeply by that conversation. He was also moved when God later said, "Tell them everything that I will do to them, but don't expect them to listen. Cry out your warnings, but don't expect them to respond" (Jeremiah 7:27). Seeing the unresponsiveness of the people he cries, "Oh, that my eyes were a fountain of tears; I would weep forever; I would sob day and night for the slain of my people! Oh, that I could go away and forget them and live in some wayside shack in the desert, for they are all adulterous, treacherous men" (Jeremiah 9:1, 2).

The Israelites scoffed at Jeremiah. Pashur, the priest in charge of the temple of the Lord, even arrested Jeremiah and had him whipped and put in stocks. Then Jeremiah complained. "If I say I'll never again mention the Lord— never more speak in his name—then his word in my heart is like fire that burns in my bones, and I can't hold it in any longer" (Jeremiah 20:9).

The word became like fire in Jeremiah's bones because he had to speak what the people didn't want to hear. This kind of fire burned the more hotly in Jeremiah because he was challenged publicly by a false prophet denying the very words of prophecy that Jeremiah had given. Jeremiah had to contradict the false prophet in the name of the Lord of hosts. He said to him, "Listen, Hananiah, the Lord has not sent you, and the people are believing your lies. Therefore the Lord says you must die. This very year your life will end because you have rebelled against the Lord" (Jeremiah 28:15, 16). Two months later Hananiah died.

Such a message can be given only if without a doubt one has heard the word of the Lord clearly. Then he can also say with Jeremiah, "But the Lord stands beside me like a great warrior, and before him, the Mighty, Terrible One, they shall stumble. They cannot defeat me; they shall be shamed and thoroughly humiliated, and they shall have a stigma upon them forever" (Jeremiah 20:11). Such a man speaks with a fire of God within his bones.

I remember so well when the words of God were like fire in my own bones. I was compelled to speak them. The church where I was pastor was at a point of crisis, as Israel was in Jeremiah's day. Churches go through times of crisis, as individuals in their growth. We do not grow by smooth progress only. We come to tests in which we have to take stock and decide whether we will go on or not. If we risk further progress and get through the trial we may be on a plateau for a while again. The church I pastored at that time was at such a point, where we were called to go on. Some were eager to do so, but some wanted to keep the status quo. The issue had to be faced, for the church could no longer "halt between two opinions."

I sought the Lord earnestly for the message to give to the church for the occasion. The Lord did not give it to me through good logic or sermons. Instead he promised me words to say at the appointed time. When they came, they were like the fire with which Jeremiah spoke. They were not thought up, nor could they easily be restrained. They burned and I had to let them out. In the hearts of the hearers they had the same effect. To those who loved the Lord and his Word, they were like the fire that cleanses and purifies. To those who resisted the Lord, they were like the fire that heats the metal and burns the chaff. As human pastors we only lay the wood; the fire is from the Lord. That is how the Word of God is when his Spirit puts it to flame.

At times God speaks in his "still small voice." Elijah may well have expected God to send thunder from heaven after he had proved before Ahab that God was alive. But then Jezebel threatened to kill him, and Elijah fled for his life. At Mount Horeb God called Elijah out of the cave in which he lived in his discouragement, to stand on the mountain while the Lord would pass by. First there came a mighty wind but the Lord was not in the wind. Then there was an earthquake but the Lord was not in the earthquake. Then there was a fire but the Lord was not in the fire. "And after the fire, there was the sound of a gentle whisper. When Elijah heard it, he wrapped his face in his scarf and went out and stood at the entrance of the cave" (1 Kings 19:12, 13). Then the voice of the Lord spoke to him in a whisper.

Elijah proved to Jezebel and all her idolatrous priests that his God was the God who controls the rain and will send it or withhold it at his will. The demonstration showed that Elijah's God can make the fire fall from heaven. But now that that task was over, Elijah had to be quiet and listen to what God was saying to *him*. There are times when God speaks to us in the still small voice or gentle whisper.

I remember such an occasion in my own life. We had returned from a four-month lecture tour in South America and Africa, and were eager to get home again. However, our furniture had been stored before we left, and we did not have a home to go to. We began to look in the area of the church to which we had been led. We looked and looked for a home, but found nothing. The requirements for the home we needed were rather specific in view of our ministry and travel. But even when we found a suitable house we had no sense of freedom from the Lord to settle on it. A year and a half had gone by without a home. Lillie was getting weary of the continual packing and unpacking.

Then one day as I was driving to look at another house, already feeling that this was not going to be the house for us, I clearly "heard" a still small voice. The Lord was asking me a question. "Do you know what kind of house you want?" he asked. "No," I replied, "not exactly." Then again the silent voice deep within me said, "Did I not give you exactly the kind of car you asked for?" I had to say, "Yes." In fact the car was so exactly what I'd asked for, in condition, color, and size as well as accessories, that I even wished I'd added one or two more items!

I knew that this was the still small voice of the Lord speaking to me. When I returned home, Lillie and I talked and prayed over our house needs. We considered every room of the house. We wrote down what we needed, including the right general location, and the care and maintenance of the house when we were away. We also considered the privacy needed after returning from the times of ministry.

Within a matter of days, we found the house. The living room was large enough to accommodate guests. Even the fireplace that we wished for but did not insist on was there. There were extra bedrooms and a bath for guests as well as for ourselves. Lillie had an adequate kitchen—even more than we had hoped for. I had a beautiful paneled study. There was sufficient storage space and it was on private property with a manager to maintain and protect it. I had hoped for a half acre of woods for my private restoration. The Lord arranged for a house that was on the edge of a ten-thousand-acre tract of state land. Every room had picture windows looking out on the beautiful scenery. I believe God must have been trying to tell us earlier, but we could not hear his gentle whisper while we were rushing about and looking.

God speaks and we can hear him. Sometimes his voice is like a trumpet blast. Sometimes like the roar of a lion. Sometimes like fire in our bones. And often like a still small voice. Whatever way God speaks, it is vital that we learn to listen to his voice.

10
Learning
to Recognize
the Voice
of God

According to an often-told story, a young man who wanted to serve the Lord had a vision in which he saw the letters "P-C" written in the sky. He went to his pastor with the conviction that these letters meant "Preach Christ," but when the pastor looked at the farm boy he said, "No, son, they mean "Plow Corn." The story illustrates the fact that one should not go into the ministry with a questionable calling. Some persons have made that mistake. However, that does not mean that we cannot hear God's call. The Bible leaves us in no doubt that God wants to communicate with all his children, and he expects us to learn to understand him.

In the Scriptures we find the record of the experiences of many men and women who have heard God's call. The Spirit of God has woven together these narratives to give us a pattern by which we can judge our experiences. We must learn to listen to the same Spirit who guided these men and women, so that we may be in harmony with them.

However, as we begin to listen we must direct our whole attention to God. If we have opened any doors to Satan through the occult, and particularly if we have engaged in any of the kinds of evil practices that ruined the nations around Israel, we must confess these sins to God so that he can take away any advantage that Satan may have gained over us. God said, "No Israeli may practice black magic, or call on evil spirits for aid, or be a fortune teller, or be a serpent charmer, medium, or wizard, or call forth the spirits of the dead" (Deuteronomy 18:10, 11). Before we begin to open our inner beings to the spiritual realm we must renounce the devil and his deceitful ways.

Beside this, we must lay aside all prejudice, whether it be personal, racial, class, or doctrinal. Even the philosophy and theology that we have adopted may itself have walls that enclose it, keeping us from accepting ideas that are broader than the wisdom of the philosopher or the insight of the theologian. We need to learn all we can of that which is good, but submit that knowledge to God for his direction or use.

How then do we recognize the voice of God? We know that the men of God heard it differently. How does it come to us today? Sometimes that voice may come as a thought, an impression, a feeling, or a still small voice. At other times it may be like a lion's roar, shouting out God's command. Sometimes it may be like a fire in our bones that cannot be contained, so that we are impelled to speak it forth. Sometimes the word of God will be like the great wind that the Psalmist describes, felling men into repentance. Sometimes it will be like the seed falling to the ground and springing forth into life. We cannot confine the voice of God to any regular form of expression. In fact, when we begin to describe that voice in any one form we may find it eludes us. How often we have tried to pattern our hearing after someone else's and then become discouraged because we did not hear God *that way*. We must remain open to any form of expression which God may choose.

One of the problems in hearing from God is that the Holy Spirit's voice is not recognized by our senses or reason but by our spirit. It is in the spiritual realm that we hear it, whatever overtones we may or may not hear with one or more of our five senses or with our reason or our emotions. We know how at times we sense the presence of God, even though outwardly there is little or no manifestation of it. At other times we sense the subtle influence of the evil one, even though the outward expression seems very religious. It is our spirit that recognizes the difference.

Such discernment indicates that our spirit must have been awakened by the Spirit of God. Spiritual discernment is not a superficial act, but rather a deep experience of the heart. "He who is united to the Lord becomes one spirit with him" (1 Corinthians 6:17 RSV). God's Spirit relates to our spirit in the deep unconscious part of our personality, our "heart." His voice is the voice of the same Spirit of God that we first heard when we opened our lives to Christ. This is the voice which became known to our spirit when we became children of God not just in theory or doctrine but by experience. "For His Holy Spirit speaks to us deep in our hearts, and tells us that we really are God's children" (Romans 8:16).

This voice from God's Spirit to ours may be picked up by our soul through our emotions, our reason, or our intuition. We know that the voice of God may either thrill our emotions or sober us in correction. It may either give our reason much to ponder or it may suddenly enlighten it. It may challenge our will to yield to a command of God. Sometimes the voice of God brings an involuntary response from deep within. It is like the call of the mother hen gathering her chicks together. The voice of the enemy, on the other hand, may be like the whistle of the hawk that silences all the birds in fear.

Each person must learn for himself how to recognize the voice of God. That voice seems to be imprinted on the Christian's spirit as the voice of his mother is imprinted on his memory. You learned your mother's voice as you heard it over and over again from birth. While all human voices have some things in common, each is also distinct from all others. It is this distinction that we recognize. In a similar way our spirit heard the voice of the Spirit of God when he began to speak to us and gradually we have learned to recognize it.

After our conversion many of us lost that recognition of the voice of God, however. We once listened to it but then, influenced by the philosophy of this western world, we came to feel that it is not safe to follow such voices. The man who has followed only rules or laws that his reason can understand, or that his emotions can respond to, has not yet learned to walk by faith in the realm of the Spirit. This does not mean that we are not to use our minds or our emotions, but that they must be subject to our spirits as they are guided by the Spirit of God. In the spiritual realm the spirit is uppermost, while in the natural realm the mind or emotions are uppermost. People have slipped into error in seeking to listen to the voice of the Spirit of God when they have not submitted their minds and emotions to God also.

I was once afraid to listen to the voice of God because of rational thinking. I remember how I had first listened to the Spirit when I yielded myself to him in my college days. Then through the influences of rationalism I began to doubt whether what I heard was really the voice of God. Having doubted, I failed to obey—and finally almost lost that recognition. It was then that I had to come to God and ask him to teach me to recognize his voice again. I told the Lord that I was willing to venture and to make small mistakes, but I asked him to save me from big ones.

We never learn without trial and error, and that involves the willingness to risk making mistakes while seeking to do the right thing. It is safe to make mistakes with God. Remember that the psalmist says, "The steps of good men are directed by the Lord. He delights in each step they take. If they fall it isn't fatal, for the Lord holds them with his hand" (Psalms 37:23, 24). This demands a trust in God much like the trust that a little child places in his mother when he begins to walk. As he takes his first step and falls, he is not scolded. Instead mother delightedly runs to the father to tell him of their little one's accomplishment.

When we start to walk in obedience to God's voice, our heavenly Father is delighted, too. He knows that we will make mistakes, but he is glad that we have ventured. So he is willing to forgive us and teach us further. In fact, we cannot learn without the risk of making mistakes when we are trying. One does not learn to ride a bicycle without lifting his feet off the ground and pedaling. We cannot learn to swim without plunging into the water. If we want to learn to recognize the voice of God we must start by obeying that which we think God is saying to us. If we are wrong he will correct us.

Isaiah says, "And if you leave God's paths and go astray, you will hear a Voice behind you say, 'No, this is the way; walk here" (Isaiah 30:21). This implies that we are walking and not standing still. It suggests that while we are on the way doing what we think is right, but inadvertently turn aside, God will correct us. What a wonderful consolation! Therefore, it should be our desire to learn to hear and be willing to obey the voice of God.

It is also necessary that we yield our minds, our emotions, and our wills to God, so that we may not be misguided by erring human reason. We read that this happened to Joshua and the elders of Israel when God had told them not to make any treaty with their close neighbors. The people of nearby Gibeon had devised a plan to save themselves from destruction. They sent messengers dressed in worn-out clothing, riding donkeys with old saddlebags carrying remnants of old foodstuffs, to the leaders of Israel saying that they had come from a far country. When they were examined about the reason for their coming, they said that they had heard of Israel's victories over other nations and therefore they had come to sign a peace treaty with them. Finally Joshua and the other leaders believed them. "They did not bother to ask the Lord, but went ahead and signed a peace treaty. And the leaders of Israel ratified the agreement with a binding oath. Three days later the facts came out—these men were close neighbors" (Joshua 9:15, 16).

Should we then not trust our five senses and our reason? Certainly we should, but not as our sole guide. Our reason, emotions, and will must be submitted to God for him to use as he chooses. It is just as dangerous to completely reject the evidence of our natural faculties as to reject our spiritual ones. All must be yielded to him.

A personal message may come to us from God when we are reading or meditating upon the Scriptures. We may suddenly find that the experience of a Bible character shows us what we are to do in our own situation. Or a word may stand out from others as the Spirit of God seems to say, "This is for you." Or the very tenor of a passage of Scripture may change our thinking so that we can hear God say that we have made a mistake or that we are to go in a different direction.

As we hear God say something to us we must begin to act on it. The voice of God demands obedience. If we are not sure whether it was God's voice, then we may ask for confirmation. That confirmation may come through further reading of the Scripture or through word from another person, or possibly, through a sign from the Lord. God is quite willing to confirm to us his will. In the book of Judges we find that Gideon wasn't sure of the angel that appeared to him, so he asked for confirmation. "If it is really true that you are going to help me like that, then do some miracle to prove it! Prove that it is really Jehovah who is talking to me." So Gideon went home and prepared a young goat for an offering. The angel told him to place the offering on a rock. When Gideon had followed these instructions, the angel touched the meat and bread with his staff, and fire flamed up from the rock and consumed them. Then, just as suddenly, the angel was gone.

When Gideon realized that it was the Angel of the Lord, he cried out, "Alas, O Lord God, for I have seen the Angel of the Lord face to face." Then the Lord replied, "It's all right. Don't be afraid! You shall not die." (See Judges 6:17-23.)

This confirmation by the miracle satisfied Gideon for the time. But when he got a further assignment he said to God, "If you are really going to use me to save Israel as you promised, prove it to me in this way: I'll put some wool on the threshing floor tonight, and if in the morning, the fleece is wet and the ground is dry, I will know you are going to help me." That night it happened just as he had asked. But Gideon was still not absolutely sure of himself so he asked for the same sign in reverse. "Please don't be angry with me, but let me make one more test: this time let the fleece remain dry while the ground around it is wet!" Once again the Lord did as he asked. (See Judges 6:36-40.)

God was not angry with Gideon for asking him for these three signs. Instead, he even encouraged him to ask for another sign when he went to battle. "If you are afraid, first go down to the camp alone—take along your servant Purah if you like—and listen to what they are saying down there! You will be greatly encouraged and be eager to attack!" (Judges 7:10, 11). Gideon went down to the enemy line and heard a dream that encouraged and prepared him for battle. The Lord was quite willing to give him all the signs he needed to confirm his guidance. It is also evident that God wants to confirm his will to us.

The Lord demonstrated this same principle with Isaiah and King Ahaz. The king did not believe that God would protect him so God sent a message to him through Isaiah. " 'Ask me for a sign, Ahaz, to prove that I will indeed crush your enemies as I have said. Ask anything you like, in heaven or on earth.' But the king refused. 'No,' he said, 'I'll not bother the Lord with anything like that' " (Isaiah 7:11, 12). God was angry with Ahaz—angry because Ahaz was not willing to ask for a sign to prove that God would do what he promised. God felt somewhat as we feel when someone will not believe us when we try to assure him that we will do our part.

However, one day when some people asked Jesus for a sign he replied that no sign would be given them except that of the prophet Jonah. And in another instance when people demanded, "Do a miracle for us. Make something happen in the sky. Then we will believe in you," Jesus "sighed deeply when he heard this and he said, 'Certainly not. How many more miracles do you people need?' " (Mark 8:11, 12).

Why wouldn't Jesus give them any other sign? Because he had given them ample proof in all of his miracles and they needed no further sign. That principle applies to us too. If we need a sign, God is quite willing to give it, but if we do not obey that which God gives us, then God will refuse to give us another sign. If we are honestly seeking to know the will of God with a desire to do it, then God is quite willing to confirm his word, even with a sign if necessary. At times it may be his will for us to inquire from God what sign we should ask for, and he may direct us in this too. God is eager for us to know his will.

But obedience is a key to knowing God's will. Jesus said, "If any man will do his will, he shall know of the doctrine, whether it be of God, or whether I speak of myself" (John 7:17 KJV). We will soon be confused about the will of God if we do not obey what we know. We will vacillate. Things will go out of focus. On the other hand, nothing will bring guidance into focus better than obedience.

Even if we only think that we are doing it right but are sincerely mistaken concerning our guidance, we will still learn from the experience. At times I have fallen flat on my face because I ventured in a direction which I thought was the will of God but it proved not to be. I hadn't checked it carefully enough. But even so, I was better off than if I had not ventured. I at least learned that this was not the voice of God or the will of God for me. Without venturing I would have learned nothing. Proverbs 24:16 says, "Don't you know that this good man, even though you trip him up seven times, will each time rise again?" If we keep in close fellowship with the Lord, he will keep us from the big mistakes while we learn in the little things. Praise God for his wonderful grace!

It is good to share with someone else in this learning experience. Spouses and other partners in work may share their problems and then listen to God together, for there is added safety in such sharing. Often Lillie and I have shared a problem, read Scriptures that may apply to the situation, prayed, then listened. When one of us receives a "word" from the Lord we wait to see whether the word that the other receives confirms the message. Often the message Lillie received was quite different from what I received, and it sometimes came in a different way. Yet, when we were both in fellowship with the Lord, he often confirmed what one heard by the other's message. If it is not confirmed, we do not proceed. This is a process of testing what we get from the Lord.

On a larger scale a group listening experience is valuable and usually safe, if the group is in fellowship with the Lord, and with one another. There are two requirements. First it is necessary to have enough freedom in the group to let each one express what he or she "hears" or "sees." So often one will say, "I don't know if this means anything, but I think I heard God say so and so. . . ." Another says, "I know this sounds foolish, but this is what I saw." We must trust each other enough to share the slightest suggestion. The second rule is equally important. We must be honest enough to submit our guidance to the group for testing. As we'll see later, no one can afford to take his guidance from the Lord for long without having it tested by others. With these two conditions, a group of people can learn how to listen to God effectively.

An early experience of group listening taught us some important lessons. We were at a time of great crisis, and we needed the help and direction of the Lord. Just at that time we met a man who told us about his prayer group. The members of his group were well disciplined, having met together once a week for about five years. I asked permission to attend a meeting of the group. Our friend told us we were welcome, for they never invited anyone, nor told anyone to stay away; but they trusted God to bring those whom he wanted.

When we arrived, we were unknown to all but the one friend. The group gathered in a very informal manner, some sitting on the floor and some in chairs. I offered to share my request for prayer. One of the men suggested that it was better that we did not do so. This was surprising. I had never been to a prayer meeting like that before. After informal conversation stopped, some began to read the Scriptures, some were quiet in meditation and some offered audible prayer. Then one of the women had a vision. It was a vision of a belt that had many fancy ornaments to it. She did not know what the vision represented. Then a man, after prayer, told us what the vision meant. We were told to let go of that which we were holding on to. Before the evening was over we were told just what we should do the next evening, and how we should conduct ourselves.

God gave us great peace about the direction that had come from the group. However, the group members who spoke these words to us did not know what our need was until we told them. Then they said, "You can see now, how much better it is that you did not tell us your problem. In this way you can see for yourself that it is God who has spoken to you through us."

They also pointed out that one had a vision, one a Scripture, one a word, while another of the members never received direction in this way. However, the confirmation that each gave was essential. In fact, if there was not unity within the group, they would not proceed with any action. The word that they gave us proved to be wise direction for the next evening. Other parts of the prophecy are still being carried out. That which they suggested would happen came to pass just as indicated, and we are still anticipating the promise of good things yet to come. This experience became a real example to us of what God can do through a group that is disciplined and willing to listen to God.

There are other lessons to be learned. This was clearly illustrated in an experience with a small group in Canada. We had been without a house to live in for over a year. Living in other people's homes in the course of our ministry, we were eagerly looking for the possibility of getting settled. At that time I was giving a series of lectures in a beautiful part of Ontario, surrounded by rich rolling farm lands with houses nestled in the woods. As we drove through the country, we would say, "Isn't that a beautiful setting for a house?" Or: "Wouldn't it be nice to live there?" One day very near the end of our ministry in that area, the pastor called from our church over two hundred miles away, saying that they had found just the house for us. They felt sure it was that which God wanted us to have. In fact, they were so sure, that they did not want to lose it and offered to have a small plane come and pick us up to show us the house and take us back again for the last two days of our ministry.

When we heard it, we were quite doubtful within our own selves. However, we were willing to consider the offer. But at that very time I was with a group of about fifty people studying about listening to God. In the discussion hour I told them that I had a project for them. I presented the request of our pastor and asked if they would listen to God to help us determine whether this was the house for us or whether we should take up the pastor's offer to fly over to see the house and then come back to finish our ministry. The group was quite willing to consider it. We asked the Lord to direct our thoughts and protect us from the intrusion of the evil one. Then we were quiet for about five minutes, after which I asked the people to share what they had received.

Overwhelmingly the words that came to them said to wait. They gave us statements like these: "In quietness and confidence shall be your strength," "The Son of Man has not a place to lay his head," "Except the Lord build a house, they labor in vain who build it," "God shall supply every need," "Commit yourself unto the Lord and he shall bring it to pass," "God does not usually rush us into things," "Simply trusting him day by day." The sum of their statements clearly confirmed to us that we were not to rush away to see the house.

As we learn to listen we will recognize that there are many things that crowd into our thinking that are not necessarily of the Lord, nor of the evil one; they are simply things of self with which we are occupied. In this case, there were pictures and words that we were not sure of. "A ranch type house with a red color." Then "a white house fading out of the picture." Both of these were later fulfilled. However, at the time we did not consider them seriously for they were not confirmed. In two cases there were also visions of flags on a flagpole; but they could not tell just what color the flag was, suggesting perhaps, that it might be Canadian or American.

Then a husband came to tell us that his wife had a vision she was reluctant to share. We talked to her privately. She said she saw a vision that might indicate where we should be living. She saw a big, beautiful, green maple tree that completely filled her vision. She could hardly look around it, though she tried and tried. Finally, however, she did and behind it she saw the Lord. To her, this vision seemed to indicate that it might be telling us that we ought to live in Canada since the maple leaf is Canada's emblem. However, as soon as she told me the vision, I knew what it meant. To me it said: "Canada has so filled your vision that you can't see the Lord anymore."

Both principles here are important. We had clear confirmation about our inner feeling that we were not to rush away to see the house that had been selected for us. This came from many sources. The other principle is that the one for whom the vision is given is the one who will finally know its meaning. The group was praying for us and so we were to decide on the final meaning. The vision or the word of the Lord is a confirmation of that which we already sense, though we may not be able to express it. It is very important that we do not accept the interpretation of a word or vision that someone gives us if our own hearts do not respond to it. It is also important not to force a message of prophecy or direction, or interpretation of a vision or dream upon another whose heart does not answer to it. Let the Spirit of God confirm his word to their hearts and let it be without our pressure.

So there is safety in group listening. Of course, it is possible for a group to become just as rigid as an individual. When the same group has been meeting for a long time and has been receiving helpful guidance, it is in danger of believing that they have found the correct and only way of receiving guidance. It is therefore just as important that the group submit to the larger church for correction as it is for the individual to submit to a group. This is the way the writings of that which we now call the Scriptures were first of all recognized by the ones to whom they were written. Then gradually they were recognized by the larger church as well.

God is more than willing to teach us how to hear his voice if we cooperate in faith, believing that God can speak to each of us, and in humility, being willing to submit our guidance for test. Then we can expect to find communication with God that is reliable. All guidance must be tested, for we are only learning to communicate in the spiritual realm.

11
Testing
the Voice
of God

Once we've been persuaded that we, like men of old, can hear God speak, we then run into the danger of believing that all that we hear is from God. Or we may believe that we hear the voice of God perfectly. We don't. There is One who did: Jesus, the Son of Man. But Jesus never sinned. Until we come to his perfection we will always need to test our "hearing" and our "seeing."

Too much is involved to leave the accuracy of that voice to chance. While it is true that God's voice guides obedient listeners today as it did in Bible times, yet too often we hear reports of groups that have heard God tell them to sell their homes and businesses to wait for Christ to come, or to do some other weird thing. We also find some in the mental hospital who say that God has told them that they are his prophets or messengers. So for the sake of our testimony to the world as well as our own spiritual safety, we must test what we claim to hear from God. This is the negative side of the question.

The positive side is this. His word to us needs to be tested also for the sake of preservation of that which God has given us. Samuel "let none of the words of God fall to the ground." There was a dearth of hearing from God in those days. Today also the world in its natural hopelessness, with all the wars and crime and suffering, longs for a word that transcends the natural. A church without a fresh word from the Lord runs along a dry channel of tradition. We say we are in a rut, which is very similar to a grave. How desperately we seek a word from God when our troubles have brought us to the very end of ourselves, that is, the end of our wisdom, our courage, our hope. A word from God is worth more than money can buy, and more than food itself, at such times.

There was a time of severe testing in our lives when suddenly a great trial came upon us with one of our children. We had to find the answer from the Lord. Nothing else mattered, nothing else interested us. Food was forgotten and sleep did not want to come. It was then that God gave me a personal promise that has stood with me for fifteen years. It was from the Psalms. Lillie also found her encouragement as God spoke to her from John 11:40, KJV: "Said I not unto thee that if thou wouldest believe thou shouldest see the glory of God?" Suddenly Jesus' word to Martha became God's word to Lillie, and it brought life and hope. We praise God for such words. We know they will be fulfilled though we do get impatient, for our clocks are not yet set to God's timing.

We need to test what we hear because of the very nature of our hearing. We may have the idea that we hear God just as clearly as we hear another person. But we do not even hear each other well. How much less are we apt to hear God correctly! We hear God, not with our physical ears, but with our spirits. No matter how audible a voice is, what determines whether the voice is God's, is not its loudness. Rather, one's spirit needs to be *tuned* to the Spirit of God. We know so little of the human spirit. We have much to learn about its hearing ability. In fact, we marvel that we are able to hear

God at all, for he is eternal, immortal, invisible. He is Spirit while we are physical. Yet, like most of us who can hear the radio and watch television without knowing much about how either instrument works, so it is marvelous that without much understanding we can begin to hear God. However, this demands that we test what we do hear.

Another reason for testing what we hear is that so few of us know the Scriptures well. Many are so easily swayed by different interpretations of Scripture. The same Holy Spirit who has given us the Scriptures is the One who correctly interprets these Scriptures to us. Therefore we need to be careful to check with God's principles that are borne out in the Scriptures.

John the apostle tells us that there were false teachers, and that the way to test their message, to find out whether the Holy Spirit had given it, was to ask, "Does it really agree that Jesus Christ, God's Son, actually became man with a human body? If so, then the message is from God. If not, the message is not from God but from one who is against Christ, like the 'Antichrist' " (1 John 4:2, 3).

Satan will try to imitate the voice of God. But there are two ways to recognize the enemy. As John tells us above, we can recognize him by his attitude toward Jesus Christ, for Satan will not admit that Jesus has really come from God and become man. And the other way to recognize the enemy is through the gift of discernment given us by the Spirit of God. The Spirit within us recognizes the evil spirit even though the spirit may speak deceptively beautiful words.

But how do we test the voice of *God* as it comes through man? The apostle Paul has given us a basic principle to follow. "Of the prophets, two or three may speak, while the rest exercise their judgment upon what is said" (1 Corinthians 14:29 NEB). To "exercise judgment" here means to investigate, to interrogate, or determine. Paul said also, "Do not smother the Holy Spirit. Do not scoff at those who prophesy, but test everything that is said to be sure it is true, and if it is, then accept it" (1 Thessalonians 5:19-21). Therefore the church must learn to test the word that comes to it through its members.

Scripture suggests three phases of tests: an individual test, a test by the local and the larger church, and then a test by the church universal. Each of these tests checks our relationship with Jesus Christ, our relationship to the local church, and our relationship to the church at large.

The individual test is suggested by Paul in his letter to the Colossians: "And let the peace of Christ rule in your hearts, to which indeed you are called in one body" (Colossians 3:15 RSV). To let the peace of Christ rule is to let it govern or arbitrate. The peace of God is a gift that Jesus promised. "I am leaving you with a gift—peace of mind and heart. And the peace I give isn't fragile like the peace the world gives. So don't be troubled or afraid" (John 14:27). As Jesus said, this kind of peace is unavailable from the world. It is a precious gift to the followers of the Lord Jesus Christ. It is related to the gift of the Holy Spirit.

When we are in fellowship with God this peace guards our hearts and minds. As Paul says, "If you do this you will experience God's peace, which is far more wonderful than the human mind can understand. His peace will keep your thoughts and your hearts quiet and at rest as you trust in Christ Jesus" (Philippians 4:7). The promise here is that the peace will guard hearts and minds. The word *guard* suggests protection by guards at the gates. God's peace will protect both our hearts' (our *deep unconscious*) and our minds' (our *conscious*) thoughts. Now Paul says that we are to let that peace reign—arbitrate—in our hearts. God knew that it would not be easy for us always to know whether the word that we heard was from him or from ourselves. So he gives confirmation at times as he gave it to Jeremiah when he thought he had a word from the Lord, but was assured when the word was confirmed. (See Jeremiah 32:6.)

Disobedience or unbelief will deprive us of peace. If we follow a voice that is not God's, peace will begin to leave us. That will be a signal that something is wrong. God's peace within us is a sign that we are following the right guidance. However, we dare not go long without checking our guidance with others. An explorer will not venture into the unknown long without checking his compass. We may hear a word from the Lord that may be hard to distinguish, or we may get a word that is very important, or that applies not only to us but to others. For these words especially, we need a further discernment. Therefore, Paul tells us, "Of the prophets two or three may speak, while the rest exercise their judgment upon what is said" (1 Corinthians 14:29 NEB).

How can the church do this? First of all the church that we speak of here is that part of the body of Christ that we relate to. To function as a discerning body, a church must be in submission to the Lord and his work. It must also be in harmony with itself, for the Spirit of God cannot be heard in the midst of confusion and rivalry. When we find a part of the body of Christ that is in obedience to the Lord and in fellowship with one another, we can take our guidance to that group for testing. The same Spirit is in us as is also in the membership of that body. These members can listen to the Spirit and see if he is saying the same thing to them as to us.

"But," someone asks, "why must a believer take his word of guidance to others? If the same Spirit is in them as in us, then surely he will just say the same thing anyway." It is true that the Spirit of God may well be saying the same thing to all, but we are not all hearing the same thing. As we have mentioned in an earlier chapter, we "hear" with our spirits, but our souls and bodies enter into the process. If we are physically tired, we are not as likely to respond to the word that demands action of us. And quite commonly when a person is sick he may not hear well, for he is too much occupied with his pain. That is one of the reasons we are commanded to lay hands on the sick. Others may hear the Lord better than the sick person.

But even more subtle than the physical effects on our spiritual hearing is the fact that one's whole personality enters into his hearing. Our minds, our emotions, and our wills all affect our spiritual hearing. The very logical thinker tends to believe that if a word sounds reasonable, it is most likely of the Lord. Churches are often run by that kind of thinking because some boards are composed largely of successful businessmen whose approach is very rational.

Then others are highly influenced by their emotions, at one time excited about doing great things and at other times discouraged over the slightest problem. Some may be influenced by their feelings to the extent that they cannot do anything without consulting the feelings of others. It is good to have such sensitivity, but when it keeps us from expressing ourselves, it may also keep us from hearing the Lord properly.

Some observe the natural realm so intently that they have difficulty in seeing the spiritual realm. The sensory person may see so many things that he can soon imagine all kinds of difficulties. Fears then hinder him from receiving God's word accurately.

But the strongly intuitive type of person may think that he is the one that really hears God. Elijah was probably one of that kind. He heard what others could not hear, but when he thought that he was the only one who heard God speak, God reminded him that there were still seven thousand others who had not bowed the knee to Baal. Along with all the potential of the intuitive there are also real dangers. We are all in the process of maturing. We are not yet fully balanced. But when our personality is not fully developed our hearing may be incorrect. This risk applies equally to persons with strongly developed powers of reason, emotion, or sensory faculties as well as intuition.

For this reason and for other reasons we are to submit guidance, even prophecy, to the church for discernment. In that body there will be differences of personality and together they can come to a balanced judgment. In the church there will also be discernment of evil forces that the individual may not be acquainted with. Therefore this too provides protection. All these faculties need to be exercised. The word of the book of Hebrews to the immature Christian applies here. "For everyone who lives on milk is unskilled in the word of righteousness for he is a child. But solid food is for the mature, for those who have their faculties trained by practice to distinguish good from evil" (Hebrews 5:13, 14 RSV).

Along with the test of the local there is the test of the larger church. This we may do by going beyond our local church or denomination, for denominational doctrines sometimes hem us in. It is of great value for us to listen to Christians of a different doctrinal background who also submit themselves to Jesus Christ. It is the Spirit of God who points out lessons for us to learn from those of different background who also really know the Lord. The Spirit of God also within us witnesses to the Spirit in them.

We have been divided among the denominations for so many years. Do we dare to think that God has taught only us and not others the great truths of the Christian life? Certainly he has been teaching all who have submitted themselves to Jesus Christ, in one way or another. How refreshing it is to spend time in discussion and quiet meditation and prayer with those of other doctrinal persuasion, and to listen to God through them. We benefit as we see things from a different perspective. This kind of correction is desperately needed. God has hidden nuggets of truth in all believers. When we listen and share we find those nuggets. Without this kind of balance we may interpret a word from the Lord with too much of the bias of our own tradition. Praise God that he, by his Spirit, brings us together so that we can listen to each other.

God is a God of order and not of confusion. But he is not subject to *our* order, either of class, race, doctrine or philosophy. He has a higher order, crossing all the boundaries we make. God's point of view is something like that which we perceive as we fly around the world. It is just one world, though it has been cut into many nations, each defending and fighting over its own boundary. Similarly, God has his universal truth, but it has been divided up by many denominations, each defending its own doctrines. We are to submit to God's order so that if he speaks a word to us, that word may be tested not by our prejudices but by the overall pattern laid out for us in the Scriptures.

Beyond the individual tests and the tests of the local

church and the larger church there is the experience of the church universal. The experiences of believers over thousands of years has been congealed in the form that we now know as the Scriptures. Here are many varied experiences of mankind gathered together in one book. Since the church through the ages has recognized these records and letters and songs and messages to be applicable to all, it is important for us to become acquainted with them.

Thus the study of the Scriptures is basic to our understanding of God's guidance. We must learn to study and meditate upon the Word of God. We may listen to the direct teaching and check our guidance with it. If, for instance, one of us were to get a personal word of guidance that would violate any one of the Ten Commandments, given to us by Moses, then we definitely know that we have not "heard" right. God does not contradict himself. He does not say one thing in his written commandments and then say something contradictory in private. Jesus interpreted the commandments even more fully (but never in contradiction). Therefore we listen to what Jesus has said and check our understanding with that. And besides, we have the teachings of his apostles and prophets to help direct our way. We may also take people's experiences as related in the Scriptures and compare our experiences with theirs. Therein we find the principles for guidance that are involved in the direct teaching.

Satan of course tries to deceive us by quoting Scripture out of context. When he tempted Jesus on the roof of the Temple, he said "Jump off and prove you are the Son of God; for the Scriptures declare, God will send his angels to keep you from harm, . . .they will prevent you from smashing on the rocks below." But Jesus knew that Satan was misapplying Scripture, so he answered, "It also says not to put the Lord your God to a foolish test." We need to know more of the Scriptures than simply a text to prove a point. There are principles to be found in the Word of God that we must take heed to as we walk in the way of the Lord. It is not sufficient to consider only what we think the Scripture says, but to compare it with what many others think it means, as they too have been listening to what God is saying.

To live by the Word of God we must meditate upon it in the way that God told Joshua: "Constantly remind the people about these laws, and you yourself must think about them every day and every night so that you will be sure to obey all of them. For only then will you succeed" (Joshua 1:8). Through meditation upon the Scriptures we come to understand the deeper truths that are hidden in the Word of God. In this way we come to hear God more clearly, for in the Scriptures is hidden the wisdom of God.

If industry spends years of time and millions of dollars in research in order to learn the secret laws hidden in the universe, how much more do we need to learn the spiritual laws that God has put into his Word. Jesus said concerning himself, "The Son can do nothing by himself. He does only what he sees the Father doing, and in the same way. For the Father loves the Son, and tells him everything he is doing" (John 5:19, 20). He learned the deep secrets of the Father's working and he carried them out.

We must learn to listen carefully and without fear, for God is still speaking to men. We must also examine and check our guidance so that we can in reality learn to recognize God's voice and follow him.

We test every message that we get from the Lord whether it comes by voice, vision, dream, prophecy, revelation, or otherwise. In our everyday experience we test it by the peace that God gives us as we walk honestly in his way. Then we may invite the local church to discern whether it is a true message from God or whether much of it, or even all of it, comes from ourselves. At all times we test it with the experience of the church universal by going to the Scriptures. There we can compare our little experience with the experiences of men and women of God from varied backgrounds over many centuries. In this way we will be kept from the deceit of the enemy and from the selfish desires that plague us all.

Jesus said, "My sheep hear my voice." Of those words

and of their context, John 10:19-30, J. H. Jowett of England wrote:

> *This is a spiritual discernment. We may test our growth in grace by our expertness in detecting the voice of our Lord. It is the skill of the saint to catch "the still small voice" amid all the selfish clamours of the day, and amid the far more subtle callings of the heart. It needs a good ear to catch the voice of the Lord in our sorrows. I think it requires a better ear to discern the voice amid our joys. The twilight helps me to be serious; the noonday glare tends to make me heedless.*
>
> *"And they follow Me." Discernment is succeeded by obedience. That is the one condition of becoming a saint—to follow the immediate call of the Lord. And it is the one condition of becoming an expert listener. Every time I hear the voice, and follow, I sharpen my sense of hearing, and the next time the voice will sound more clear.*
>
> *My Saviour, graciously give me the listening ear. Give me the obedient heart.*[7]

12
Hearing
the Inaudible
and Seeing
the Invisible

To hear the voice of the infinite, eternal, invisible God is a great challenge for sinful, finite man. Yet it is a wonderful fact that man can hear and learn to understand that voice. To have communication with God means for us to hear the inaudible and see the invisible. It means that we must not only have theoretical knowledge but experience in the spiritual realm.

Yet the spiritual realm is a dangerous realm because it is the realm of the unknown. It is the realm both of the Holy God and of Satan, the proud deceiver who makes his claim on us. We can only enter that realm safely with the escort that God has given to us, namely Jesus, the Son of God who entered into hell itself and overcame Satan. In Jesus' name we can have absolute victory over the enemy. We need not fear him anymore.

Even with Jesus as our escort, we must learn t'ie princi-

ples of the spiritual realm lest we leave any door open for the
enemy to slip in and deceive us. The place where we meet
God is the place where the natural and the supernatural
meet. That place is often pictured in myths and fairy tales. In
C. S. Lewis's *Narnia Tales* it is Aslan, representing Christ,
who is so really present at one time, but remains totally invisible at other times.

In the Scriptures the place where the natural and the
supernatural meet is revealed to us in the appearances of
Jesus after his resurrection. Jesus then possessed a strange-
to-us combination of the natural and the supernatural, his
spiritual body. That body could be seen and touched and
handled, but it could also appear and disappear at will. The
experiences of Jesus and his followers after the resurrection
will give us a clue as to how to handle the voices and visions
that proceed from the spiritual realm.

Where do we find the Lord so that we can recognize
him? That place is where the natural and the spiritual meet.
We find this illustrated in the experience of the two disciples
of Emmaus after Jesus' resurrection. The two were walking
to Emmaus, talking sadly of Jesus' death, when Jesus suddenly joined them though they were kept from recognizing
him. He asked them about their deep discussion. They were
surprised that he did not seem to know about the crucifixion
of the One who they had hoped was their Messiah. Then
Jesus began to explain passage after passage of Scripture
concerning himself.

That experience might have done nothing more for
them than to provide an intellectual understanding, had
they not responded to him specifically. But we read: "By this
time they were nearing Emmaus and the end of their jour-
ney. Jesus would have gone on, but they begged him to stay
the night with them, as it was getting late. So he went home
with them."

Had the disciples not begged Jesus to stay with them, he
would have gone on, it seems. It is not that Jesus needs to be
begged, but he does want to be invited. He goes only where
he is genuinely welcomed. In Revelation 3:20 John quotes
him saying, "Look! I have been standing at the door and I

am constantly knocking. If anyone hears me calling him and opens the door, I will come in and fellowship with him and he with me."

One of the first lessons that we must learn if we want to have Jesus manifest himself to us is that we must come with a deep desire to know him. He has promised satisfaction to those who come famished with hunger. He has promised rivers of living waters to flow from those who truly thirst. That is why we need to take time to wait upon him. Psalm 27:14 says, "Don't be impatient. Wait for the Lord, and he will come and save you! Be brave, stout-hearted and courageous. Yes, wait and he will help you." Our shallow interests must become deep channels of holy desire. Our hearts need to be prepared for him when he comes.

Cleopas and his companion might have missed really *seeing* their Lord if they had not urgently invited Jesus to stay with them. But as they sat down to eat, he asked God's blessing on the food and then took a small loaf of bread and broke it and was passing it over to them, when suddenly—they recognized him! And at that moment he disappeared!

Afterwards they began telling each other how their hearts had felt strangely warm as he talked with them and explained the Scriptures during the walk down the road. The disciples had set the table for him and he blessed the food. They had a natural part to do. When they did it, he brought the spiritual into the natural and they recognized him.

To use an Old Testament figure, it is necessary that we lay the wood, so that the flame from heaven can consume it. If we do not come to the Lord's table with our hearts prepared for the celebration, we may miss the revelation of Jesus' presence. And if we do not take specific time to read and meditate upon the Scriptures, the Lord may not speak to us. There is natural preparation to make for the appearance of the supernatural. Sometimes that preparation is made quite unconsciously, and the manifestation of the Lord comes as a surprise. But preparation does have to be made.

Another lesson we learn about supernatural experiences

is that we do not always recognize the Lord when he does
come. We see this in the experience of one who truly loved
him. Mary Magdalene longed to see the one who had set her
free from the evil that had bound her so long. She must have
been unable to sleep through those first nights after the terrible crucifixion of her Master. So, very early, while it was
still dark, she came to the cave tomb where Jesus had been
buried. To her amazement, the stone that had covered the
cave's entrance had been rolled away. So she ran to tell Peter
and John. They went to the tomb and saw that the body of
Jesus indeed was gone. By that time, Mary had returned to
the tomb and was standing outside crying. She saw two
angels in the tomb, who asked her why she was crying. She
told them she thought they had taken away her Lord. Then—
"She glanced over her shoulder and saw someone standing
behind her. It was Jesus but she didn't recognize him! 'Why
are you crying?' he asked her. 'Whom are you looking for?'
She thought he was the gardener" (John 20:14, 15).

Similarly, Cleopas and his companion did not recognize
Jesus when he walked with them. Jesus came in a different
guise to them. He had told them that he would come and
they would not recognize him. Now he was doing just that.

I believe that Jesus often comes to us unrecognized,
through an interruption of our schedule. Such an interruption may even happen while we are seeking to be very quiet
before him. A little child may come in, or the telephone may
ring. It is a gift from God to be able to discern when we are
to allow an interruption and when not. There were times
when Jesus sent the crowds and even the disciples away, for
he knew he had to be alone. There were other times when he
took time for the little ones even though his disciples
thought him too busy to do that. Once when some mothers
were bringing their children to Jesus, the disciples sent them
away, telling them not to bother him, but Jesus was very dis-
pleased with that action of the disciples. He said, "Let the
children come to me, for the Kingdom of God belongs to
such as they" (Mark 10:14). Our busy-ness may sometimes
be part of our pride in which we think that certain people
whom we want to see are more important than the ones God

sends to us. We may not recognize our Lord as he comes in the person of little children.

There was an interruption of another kind that Jesus turned into a great occasion. That was when Jairus, the rabbi, came to Jesus and begged him to heal his daughter, for she was dying. Jesus started to go but was interrupted by a woman who touched the edge of his robe. Jesus allowed himself the time to assure her of her healing, but it was too much time for Jairus' little daughter. The girl died in the meantime. But Jesus did not allow himself to be discouraged. He trusted in his Father's timing. He turned the "defeat" of the lost opportunity into a great resurrection victory. Our time is often not God's timing. We miss his appointments only because we think we have to get on with our own.

Coming back to Mary Magdalene at the grave of Jesus, notice that she did not recognize Jesus by sight. Then Jesus called her by name. He simply said, "Mary." It was then that she recognized his voice and exclaimed, "Master!"

What a deep emotional response that voice must have brought to her! She remembered that voice which had called her out of sin, and which had set her free, and which had encouraged her. It was the same voice and she knew it was her Lord. So it is also with us. We may not know him under strange circumstances, but his voice is familiar when he speaks to us in the relationship in which he has spoken so many times before.

When Mary recognized Jesus' voice she grabbed for him in her desire to be with him. Jesus said, "Do not cling to me, for I have not yet ascended to my Father" (John 20:17). What a shock it would have been if she had been holding on to Jesus tightly and he had suddenly disappeared. He had a real body but it was one that could appear and disappear. This is the way it is with our spiritual experiences. They are there and then as suddenly they are gone and we cannot hold on to them. The spiritual realm is manifest in the natural just long enough to encourage or to speak to us, but then we must let go of the physical evidence and walk by faith again.

People have visions or experiences like this and then try

to live by them. Their spiritual testimony is based on a revelation that God has given them for growth; but if they do not
grow thereby, the purpose is lost. As someone has said, the
fact that we have had an unusual experience does not make
us unusual. We grow to maturity through many and varied
experiences.

There are times when that presence may be terribly
frightening. Just after the breaking of the bread with Jesus,
the Emmaus disciples returned quickly to the others in
Jerusalem. The two disciples from Emmaus began telling of
their experience when they recognized Jesus in his breaking
of the bread. Luke also wrote about the time when "just
as they were telling about it, Jesus himself was suddenly
standing there among them. But the whole group was terribly frightened, thinking they were seeing a ghost!" (Luke
24:36, 37).

An earlier but similarly frightening experience is described by Matthew. "Night fell, and out on the lake the disciples were in trouble. For the wind had risen and they were
fighting heavy seas. About four o'clock in the morning Jesus
came to them, walking on the water! They screamed in terror, for they thought he was a ghost" (Mark 13:23-26). But
he reassured them, telling them not to be afraid.

Jesus may actually come so unexpectedly, in the midst of
a frightening situation, that we may think his presence is
something evil. But it is to our need that he comes, and he
wants to reveal himself, as he did to Peter, calling him to
walk on the water. This is illustrated in the account of Jesus'
appearance to the two disciples from Emmaus, along with
the others. " 'Why are you frightened?' he asked. 'Why do
you doubt that it is really I? Look at my hands! Look at my
feet! You can see that it is I, myself! Touch me and make
sure that I am not a ghost! For ghosts don't have bodies, as
you see that I do!' As he spoke he held out his hands for
them to see [the marks of the nails], and showed them [the
wounds in] his feet" (Luke 24:38-40). Then he commis-
sioned them to take his message of forgiveness to all the
world. Just at the time of need, when we may be most

frightened, he may be there to heal, or to deliver, or to bless, or to commission us.

The presence of the evil one brings fear over which we can have victory in the name of Jesus. The presence of the Lord may frighten us as he comes in his majesty and power, but he comes also with the words, "Do not be afraid." There is nothing to fear in the loving presence of our Lord as long as we are walking humbly before him. Our natural reaction because of our sinfulness may cause us to react that way, but with God there is mercy and forgiveness.

To some people all of these experiences are too nebulous. They want proof, meaning *physical* evidence. That is what Thomas did. Jesus had said to Thomas, "Put your finger into my hands. Put your hand into my side. Don't be faithless any longer. Believe!" Then you remember, Thomas exclaimed, "My Lord and my God!" Jesus then told him, "You believe because you have seen me. But blessed are those who haven't seen me and believe anyway" (John 20:27-29).

Those who refuse to believe must hurt our Lord deeply. But those who cannot believe will find help from the Lord himself for their faith, if they will ask for it. Often it is just a matter of obedience. Jesus told his disciples to believe and not to be fearful. That was a command. Faith is partly a matter of will. If we do not put faith into operation, the spiritual principles through which God works are inoperable.

Two similar experiences took place in twin towns in Canada. Just as I was about to speak in a restaurant meeting a group from a fraternal club from various parts of the country arrived. Their adjoining room was separated from our room only by a partial wall. Their greetings and renewal of acquaintance and other friendly talk made it impossible for our group to hear what we came to hear. But how could we impose our silence upon them? I debated about what I could do but felt constrained to leave the impossible with God and pray that God would bless both them and us. God answered. I was not even aware, until my attention was called to it at the end of my talk and prayer, how beautifully

God had answered. He gave an unusual quietness in both rooms. The miracle was so small, but the effect upon us all has been a reminder of the Lord's presence ever since.

About a year later, in a beautiful university building, we were given a dome room with a glass roof for our lectures on prayer. Again, just as I was about to speak, there was a roar that made it impossible to hear each other. This time it was a downpour of rain. Was it the attempt of the enemy to destroy that meeting? Or was it the presence of the Lord waiting to be invited? I was immediately reminded to ask the Lord to intervene. With the reminder came the temptation to doubt and not dare, but after we prayed the rain softened and it was beautifully quiet until the lecture was over and we had gotten to the cars. Then the downpour continued. Once again it was the Lord's presence by that answer to prayer that became so real to us.

Faith is especially needed when we are seeking to hear from God. If we have constant doubts whether God is speaking or not, we will soon find that we are not hearing or are entirely unable to discern what is the voice of God. Faith is not a vague principle. It is very practical. It represents our attitude toward God, that is, that we believe him and believe that he will do what he has promised. Faith, however, is always based upon a promise from the Lord. If we seek to have faith, but have no promise or principle of the Word of God to base it upon, it is without foundation and accomplishes nothing. But like children we can act simply and trustingly upon the Word of God.

Sometimes our inability to hear God or receive direction is the result of hiding behind a mask and not walking openly in the light. This was true of Peter at one time. After his resurrection Jesus had an assignment for Peter. However, Peter was not prepared for it. He had said that he loved the Lord more than all the rest. His pride had caused him to fall. But remember that after instituting the Lord's supper, Jesus said to them, "Tonight you will all desert me." Peter declared, "If everyone else deserts you, I won't." Jesus then told him, "The truth is that this very night, before the cock crows at dawn, you will deny me three times!" But Peter insisted, "I would die first!" (Matthew 26:31, 33-35). Then after Jesus had been taken prisoner, Peter's tests began. Three times he denied the Lord, the last time with cursing and swearing. Then Peter remembered what Jesus had said, and he went away, crying bitterly.

Even after that experience, Peter's mask was not yet removed. Peter decided to go fishing with the other disciples. That night they caught nothing. But in the morning they saw a man on shore who gave them some advice. They cast out the net as he said and soon it was full. John said, "It is the Lord!" whereupon Peter jumped into the water and swam ashore, while the others took in the net. (Peter was going to be the first to meet Jesus, even as he had implied that he loved Jesus the most.) But after breakfast, Jesus came directly to the point and asked Peter if he loved him more than the rest. He knew how he had denied the Lord before them all. Now, before them all, he had to answer the question about his love for the Lord. This time he had to do it honestly. It was not until Peter could accept his real place, that he was ready for Jesus' assignment. Once more Jesus asked him, "Simon, son of John, are you even my friend?" Peter was grieved at the way Jesus asked the question this third time, and he said, "Lord, you know my heart; you know I am." And Jesus then said, "Then feed my little sheep" (John 21:17).

We too may say that we will follow the Lord though all others leave him. Or we may make a pretense of obedience that God cannot work with. If we face ourselves honestly and correct our error, we may have a humbling experience before others. God has to deal with our pride, for pride is of the enemy and it leads to destruction.

This same problem, with unfortunate results, is illustrated in the Old Testament in the life of Saul. Saul had been chosen by God and anointed as king over Israel. But to be God's chosen servant is not simply an honor to be enjoyed. It's a charge to fulfill. Saul had been disobedient to his charge. Furthermore, he had never learned to communicate with God directly, but depended on Samuel, the prophet, who had anointed him to be king. Now the circumstances began closing in on him. The Philistines set up their camp at Shunem, and Saul and the armies of Israel were at Gilboa. When Saul saw the vast army of the Philistines, he was frantic with fear. He asked the Lord what he should do. But the Lord refused to answer him, either by dreams, or by Urim, or by the prophets. He then decided to get a message from God via a medium or witch from the forces of evil—Satan's promised shortcut. However, God intervened and brought Samuel up.

" 'Why have you disturbed me by bringing me back?' Samuel asked Saul. 'Because I am in deep trouble,' he replied. 'The Philistines are at war with us, and God has left me and won't reply by prophets or dreams, so I have called for you to ask you what to do.' But Samuel replied, 'Why ask me, if the Lord has left you and has become your enemy?' " (1 Samuel 28:15, 16). Then Samuel told him that all this had come about because of Saul's disobedience—and that he would die the next day.

That was no comforting message that came to Saul. A further historian recorded: "Saul died for his disobedience to the Lord and because he had consulted a medium and did not ask the Lord for guidance" (1 Chronicles 10:13, 14). The greater the privilege and honor that God gives us, the greater is our responsibility, and the more we need to be sure of God's guidance. The Lord does not expect us to be perfect, but he does expect us to be honest before him.

During Jesus' earthly ministry one day he told his disciples, over five hundred of them, to meet him on a mountain. Matthew says: "Then the eleven disciples left for Galilee, going to the mountain where Jesus had said they would find him. There they met him and worshipped him—but some of them weren't sure it really was Jesus!" (Matthew 28:16, 17). Some of them doubted, but he still gave them his authority. If he had had to wait until the men had no doubts at all, they would never have gone.

I remember the nights before my wife and I were to take the tour around the world. We were still eleven hundred dollars short of our fare. The dreams that came during those nights were frightening. When I asked a friend about this, he said, "Your fears are catching up with you." I replied, "I have no doubt whatsoever that God wants us to go." And he replied to me: "If you have no doubts, then I question your guidance."

Suddenly I realized that I really did have many doubts but I was 51 percent sure. So I was persuaded, in spite of my doubts, that God wanted us to go. When I faced up to my doubts and admitted them, then God's wonderful peace came back.

Surely many doubts and fears will arise in our hearts and minds as we seek to hear the inaudible and see the invisible in the spiritual realm. We will find that much of self gets involved in our communication with God. But if we are honest with ourselves and with God, he will be able to guide us. What is the veil that divides between the natural and the supernatural? Is it not usually the self that is not yet willing to risk itself to reach out for God? May we be willing to venture with God! God will prove himself faithful beyond imagination to those who put their whole trust in him and listen to his voice.

NOTES

1
Henry C. Thiessen, *Introduction to the New Testament.* (Grand
Rapids, Mich.: Eerdmans, 1943), p. 25.
2
F. F. Bruce, *Jesus and Christian Origins Outside the New
Testament* (Grand Rapids, Mich.: Eerdmans, 1947).
3
C. S. Lewis, *Reflections on the Psalms* (New York: Harcourt,
Brace, 1958), p. 97.
4
Myrna Grant, *Vanya* (Carol Stream, Ill.: Creation House,
1974), pp. 62-65.
5
H. A. Baker, *Heaven and the Angels* (Minneapolis: Osterhus,
n.d.), p. 209.
6
Op. cit., Lewis, n.p.
7
J. H. Jowett, *My Daily Meditation for the Circling Year* (London:
Clarke, 1914), p. 17.

INDEX